Lincs, Notts & Derbyshire by Rail

A guide to the routes, scenery and towns

Jarrold Colour Publications, Norwich

ABOUT THIS BOOK

In 1985 the Lincolnshire branch of the Railway Development Society published *Lincolnshire by Rail*, a rail-based guide to South Humberside and Lincolnshire. By the end of the year almost all copies were sold, demonstrating the need for a handy, readable guide to the towns, resorts and villages of these counties for the rail traveller.

The following year the East Midlands branch of the society published *Five Shires by Rail*, covering Bedfordshire, Derbyshire, Leicestershire, Northamptonshire and Nottinghamshire, and by the end of 1988 few copies remained unsold. In 1987 Jarrolds took over publishing the society's railguides and expanded the series to cover almost all of Britain.

This new book covers Derbyshire, South Humberside, Lincolnshire and Nottinghamshire. Much of the material has been updated or rewritten from the earlier books. As editor, I should like to thank all those who have contributed articles, Peter Wakefield for the map and John Brodribb for the line diagrams reproduced from the earlier books. My special thanks are due to Trevor Garrod, editor of the two previous books.

Like the other books in the series, *Lincs, Notts. & Derbyshire by Rail* has been written for the general reader. It does, however, contain some references to railway history and vocabulary. Railways in the area were mostly built in the nineteenth century by the Great Central, Great Northern, Midland, London & North Western or North Staffordshire Railway companies. All of these companies were absorbed into either the London, Midland & Scottish or London & North Eastern Railways in 1923. These – and the others of the 'big four' – were nationalized in 1948. Now there is much talk of privatising our railways, and some of the options being discussed threaten to split up the national system once again.

The 'up' track or platform is normally that used by trains heading towards London. A High Speed Train, marketed as InterCity 125, is a fast main-line diesel train with a power car at either end, capable of travelling at up to 125 mph on suitable track. 'Sprinter' is the name given to the Provincial sector's new diesel trains, introduced since 1986. Several routes in our area are served by Sprinters of the first build, with high density seating, but the Express trains to and from East Anglia have longer coach bodies and more spacious seats. Further additions to the Sprinter family in 1989/90 will introduce air conditioning and even quieter travel to several lines.

I do hope you will use this book to explore the railways of this area, and that reading and using it gives as much pleasure to you as editing it has to me.

John Saunders
March 1989

Front cover: Inter-City train, near Ambergate, Derbyshire

Back cover: Lincoln Cathedral at night

Title page: The Council House, Nottingham

CONTENTS

Nottingham Castle (*Photo:* Malcolm Goodall)

EDITOR'S INTRODUCTION

Within the area covered by this book, you can see from the train window the rocky grandeur of the Derbyshire dales, the majestic waterway of the Humber, the fertile beauty of the flat Lincolnshire fens and the bustling activity of the Nottinghamshire coalfield. Alighting from the train, you can relax at the seaside resorts of Skegness and Cleethorpes, where the beach is just forty yards from the station; glide 750 feet up from Matlock Bath by cable-car; explore the historic towns of Newark and Boston; or learn of Britain's agricultural and industrial heritage at Cromford, Scunthorpe and Heckington. You can shop in Derby, Nottingham, Lincoln – with its pedestrian area starting just outside the station, or a host of smaller towns, all worth a visit. You can walk the Pennine Way from Edale, or the Viking Way from Lincoln.

Into the area come three of British Rail's major InterCity routes. The East Coast Main Line from London and Peterborough passes through Grantham, Newark and Retford on its way to Doncaster, Yorkshire, the North East and Scotland. Its trains bring Newark within $1\frac{1}{2}$ hours of London and 2 hours of Newcastle. Increasing numbers of passengers commute regularly to London along this route, which by 1991 will be electrified through to Leeds and Edinburgh. The Midland Main Line links Sheffield, Derby and Nottingham with Leicester and London. High Speed Trains whisk you from Nottingham to London in 100–115 minutes. The traditional route from Yorkshire and the North-East to Birmingham and the West, now called Cross County InterCity, also passes through Sheffield and Derby.

Recent years have seen dramatic changes on some of the government-supported Provincial lines. Hourly Express trains now link Nottingham with Sheffield, Manchester, the north-west, Peterborough and East Anglia. Most of these trains call at Chesterfield and a few serve Derby. Until 1990 they travel through Grantham to reach Peterborough. Their journey north-westwards will be quicker as a result of a decision in January 1988 to reopen a section of line west of Nottingham for their use. There are also hourly trains from Lincoln through Nottingham and Derby to Birmingham.

All four County Councils in the area have supported their local rail services, with Lincolnshire (then Holland) the first to reopen a railway, and there are high hopes that a Nottinghamshire-led consortium will be able to restore a train service between Nottingham, Hucknall and Mansfield.

For convenience, routes are covered in broadly the order in which they appear in British Rail's passenger timetable.

John Saunders

KEY TO LINE DIAGRAMS

LUTON — Staffed station; booking office; train information available. Seats and shelter at station.

Bingham — Unstaffed station – pay on the train.

Hull — Continuous line – through trains, here shown running to the station named from the line on the diagram.
Dashed line – connecting rail service.

Station and broken line – shown for reference only. Intermediate stations and connections not shown.

PETERBOROUGH–LINCOLN via SPALDING

by John Davison

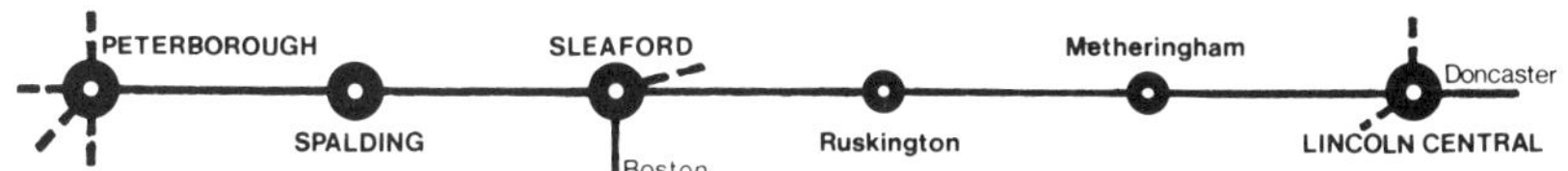

Within minutes of diverging from the main line at Werrington, your train enters Lincolnshire – a vast county where over a million sheep grazed in the mid-nineteenth century. You won't spot many on your journey nowadays.

To the east lie Peakirk Waterfowl Gardens, a haven for swans, flamingos, photographers and naturalists, five miles north of Peterborough (telephone Peterborough 252271 for details; buses from Peterborough to Bourne serve the reserve). Wildlife is now an oddity in this arable landscape.

The straight rail tracks penetrate a county where Dr William Stukely found 'true life, not the stink and noise and nonsense of London' in the mid-eighteenth century. In eastern Lincolnshire, town and country remain inseparable. The settlements ahead – Spalding, Ruskington and Metheringham – all share the suffix '-ing' reflecting the sixth-century colonisation of this area by Germanic Anglo-Saxons.

Across Deeping Fen stands Spalding, linked to the main line and Boston in 1848, to Holbeach in 1858, to Bourne in 1866, March in 1867 and Lincoln during 1882. The railway rapidly took freight from the inshore boats of the River Welland and from the unkempt boggy tracks which then linked market towns, tracks along which pack-horses towed up to a ton apiece when weather conditions allowed. Today, shrubs cannot hide the redundant platforms that remind one of those now defunct rail routes.

In 1086, Spalding's market was one of seven in the county and six fisheries were noted in the town which Ivo Tailbois, Norman Sherriff of Lincolnshire, was developing. As the centuries passed, the area bounded by Spalding, Sleaford, Boston, King's Lynn and Wisbech was embellished with numerous fine parish churches, a density of splendour unmatched elsewhere. The church bells often rang out to warn of flood or tempest.

Haughty-culture arrived in Spalding before long, a school starting in 1621 and a public library in 1637; a respected Gentlemen's Society was formed in 1710. In 1643, Royalists from Crowland raided Spalding, carrying off several supporters of Cromwell. Some improved fenland fell back to marsh during this Civil War. During the eighteenth century, regular fairs were held and industries for brewing, boatbuilding and sail-making sprang up. Great droves of cattle and geese grazed local fields *en route* to London, the growing capital, much to the annoyance of commoners. Potatoes and rape were important crops, an oil mill opening in 1816, the Pode Hole beam engine (which survives) in 1825, a bank in 1831 and a grammar school in 1837.

Towards the close of the last century, sugar beet arrived and the cut-flower market began to blossom. The ashlar land agent's office at the corner of New Road and Hall Place reflects the wealth of this era. In 1926 a sugar beet factory opened at the rear of Springfields, the summer showground for bulbs, bedding plants and roses on the A151 Holbeach road. The factory closed in 1989. Since 1959 a Saturday Flower Parade has been held early each May, for which special trains have come to Spalding from many parts of the country. Whitemoor Marshalling Yard in

March boosted rail traffic from 1928 onwards. By 1984 Spalding's population had risen above 18,200 and a tourist office had opened (telephone 5468).

On leaving J. Taylor's 1848 station, note the Chatterton Tower to your left – a high water-tower including offices for local officials! Bus timetables displayed on your right show routes to Boston, Peterborough (via Market Deeping or Crowland) and King's Lynn (via Holbeach and Long Sutton). Vacant yards and a five-storey British Telecom office provide an unappetising welcome for the sightseer.

Turn right at the public house to find a homely café called The Farmer's Wife, whose menu includes 'Pig in a Blanket', an omelette with a Lincolnshire sausage! Go left, and right past the 1842 Sessions House to find the Market Place, which frankly disappoints. Market days are Tuesday and Saturday. In 1715, a gallant ex-sailor blew up a house opposite the Old White Hart to check the spread of a serious fire. He lost his life in the process and the fire caused £20,560 worth of damage. Stone from Crowland Abbey was brought to aid rebuilding work.

Central Spalding is sadly peppered with clumsy flat-roofed shops and workshops. For reminders of a more elegant age, try Broad Street, Church Street, Double Street, Kings Road, London Road or Pinchbeck Road, all outside the shopping district. Ayscoughfee Hall, a mellow modest fifteenth-century house with a 'Tudoresque' facade of 1845, a small park and children's zoo, deserves a visit, if only to admire the stone carvings at eaves level. From outside, the adjoining parish church appears too wide and jumbled, but persist: inside the hammer-beamed roof of 1450 and the painted chancel ceiling of 1959 are marvellous. A richly detailed sixteenth-century window on the north side and the 1766 brass chandelier are also ornate. Nearby the Brush and Palette offers a colourful setting for a bite or two. The handsome houses and warehouses alongside the River Welland reflect the eighteenth-century wealth of the area. The draining of local fens not only raised crop yields but also increased the flow of water through the town and reduced the risk of heavy silting.

From a train leaving Spalding heading north, observe the old iron footbridge spanning railway land, its stairways over 60 metres apart. The 'Capital of Tulip-land' merges into Pinchbeck and fenland reappears. The wildness of these lands is often exaggerated: as early as 1591 detailed by-laws were adopted in Spalding to regulate wildfowling and to prevent hunting during the breeding season. The reclamation of marsh began in 1626 and was a social as well as a technical revolution. Fen folk, used to fishing and fowling, disliked the greed of adventurers, the rent rises and the strict discipline of arable farming. Heavy crops of corn, beans, mustard, hemp and cole-seed became available and by 1808, 200,000 acres had been reclaimed in Lincolnshire.

Eight miles from Spalding the train skirts the western edge of Donington, where the parish continues to push for a station (the original one, like most village stations on this line, having been closed in 1961). Other sites for new stations could be Pinchbeck and Helpringham.

We cross the South Forty Foot Drain, built in 1765 between the Rivers Slea and Glen, and once lined by no fewer than 63 windmills to pump the fens dry. On a clear day, away to the north-east, can be seen Boston Stump and, to the north, Heckington church and windmill.

The remote signal-box of Blotoft stands half a mile beyond the bridge, its place-name repeated on no other building or map. Next comes the village of Helpringham, on the right, dominated by the spire and pinnacles of its church tower. Through a few shallow cuttings, and your train bears left into Sleaford, crossing Mareham Lane, a Roman road, where it joins the Boston line. By 1086, Sleaford possessed eight watermills; a good water supply also led Bass to develop enormous maltings here between 1892 and 1905. These tower majestically to the

Spalding Tulip Parade. (*Photo*: Peter Cronin)

south of the railway, awaiting new users. The malting activities ceased in 1958, but two Bass pubs survive in the town.

In the early sixteenth century, Robert Carre, the King's Steward, was much criticised for letting the town of Sleaford decay and for vandalising churches and castle. The canalisation of the River Slea in 1792 was crucial for the town's revival. The first railway arrived from Grantham in 1857 and the canal company folded by 1878, just four years before the arrival of trains from Spalding. Sleaford was linked by rail to Boston in 1859 and to Bourne in 1872, the stone-built station being extended (in brick!) as new tracks boosted traffic.

Sleaford Station presents a pleasant gateway to the town, with three platforms, enhanced by thoughtful landscaping and re-lighting schemes. It is well worth pausing to admire the carefully tended garden and ornamental pool at the western end of the island platform; and the topiary work on platform one. UKF Fertilisers have a siding and warehouse opposite platform three, thankfully designed with Railfreight in mind.

The following circular walk may be enjoyed within an hour, but allow longer if you wish to feed either yourself or the local ducks. From Station Road, which has a handy café, turn left past a cinema built in 1920 to Handley's Monument. Charles Kirk, contractor for the 1882 Spalding–Ruskington line, lived in the adjacent stone mansion now forming part of the High School. Some of the pupils now travel to school by train from Heckington, Ruskington and Metheringham. An arched passageway next to the Halifax Building Society office enables you to reach the Tourist Information Centre at the base of a black mill-tower. Veer right past the town's wine bar and over an old canal bridge. Now follow the towpath past bulrushes until an old watermill is reached. Turn left into Eastgate and enjoy a striking cemetery lodge and a group of charity almshouses on your way to the re-paved Market Place. Market day is Monday. The early spire and window tracery of the adjacent parish church are much admired. Stone is also well-used along Northgate; take the passage past number 23 to discover Westholme Chateau, now used as a sixth-form centre. Turn left into Westgate and head back towards the church spire. Sleafordian Coaches, now running scheduled services on behalf of Lincolnshire County Council, have their depot here in Westgate. Don't be afraid to ask for a timetable – it's a friendly outfit. Right at the lights will set you back across the River Slea towards the station. Nine carriage archways survive along this stretch of Southgate. Sleaford, a relaxed shopping centre marred only by heavy lorries, sustained a weekly livestock market from 1868 until 1984.

Somewhat surprisingly, trains leave Sleaford Station westwards when heading to Lincoln, looping tightly within the built-up area. You will pass new factories before rejoining the track which bypasses the town to the east.

After passing under the A17 trunk road, look for the tiny church of Evedon half a mile east and await the halt at Ruskington, rebuilt and reopened in 1975. Fine examples of Victorian housing line the road from the station to the older village core, where All Saints' Church, dating from the twelfth century, awaits you. A scenic route through Ewerby and Howell to Heckington is recommended for cyclists: turn right from the station to follow this eight-mile route.

Digby station buildings, two miles north of Ruskington, now form a private home, but Metheringham, five miles further on, was reopened in October 1975 with finance largely from the County Council. About 40 commuters and many Saturday shoppers use the trains from 'Meg', and a compact trading estate has been built east of the station to broaden the range of local jobs. If you've time to explore, turn right outside the station, left by the roadside chevrons and cross to a narrow footpath. A fine prospect of the twelfth-century church appears and within St Wilfrid's a lavish marble monument survives. In 1705 the vicar here was so in debt that he hid during visitations.

Beyond the church, proceed left along the High Street, noting the cottage post-office and a good-looking Methodist church built of Blankney stone in 1907–8 to a design by A. E. Lambert. An earlier chapel of 1840 still stands opposite, now a motor showroom. Return along High Street towards the station; if you continue southwards for a mile instead, the nineteenth-century estate village of Blankney will impress. In the 1860s, farmer James Caird noted that labourers commuted six miles or more by donkey to avoid high rents charged in some villages. Commuting is clearly not a new phenomenon round here! Cyclists will find a 12-mile circuit through Blankney, Scopwick, Timberland and Martin most pleasant in fair weather. A return trip to Woodhall Spa may appeal to the more energetic.

As you leave Metheringham's northbound platform by train, you may notice a crop-spraying helicopter parked near the track, a symbol of the sophistication associated with modern farming. The railway now runs across quite high ground, with views to the east of fenland which was much improved following the raising of the Witham banks in 1762. Nocton Fen was served by a two-foot-gauge railway from 1926 to 1960, with potatoes and sugar beet being transferred via a siding to the national railway network.

We pass through limestone cuttings and then see Branston Comprehensive School on the western skyline, before the train descends a left-handed curve into Lincoln. Enjoy the prospect of the Cathedral from the right-hand windows.

While few trains use the section from Spalding to Sleaford, a more intensive service links Sleaford with Lincoln. In the daytime period, an hourly train runs between Peterborough and Spalding, a route closed to passengers in 1970, but reopened with local authority financing in June 1971, with a target of attracting 12,000 passengers a year. By 1987 some 110,000 people used the service in a year.

A walk around Lincoln is described on page 40.

LINCOLN–DONCASTER

by Cyril J. Clark

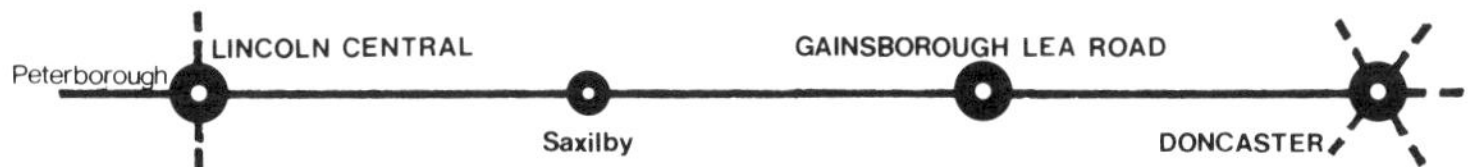

The train leaves Lincoln across the High Street level-crossing, scene of numerous incidents where impatient motorists ignore the traffic lights protecting the crossing, past another level-crossing and East Holmes signal-box, to give a clear view to the east of the majesty of Lincoln Cathedral. The line to Newark and Birmingham curves sharply away to the west, with Holmes Yard to the east. Soon it passes Pyewipe Junction, where the single-track allowing trains from Newark to bypass Lincoln converges, and from where the old Lancashire, Derbyshire & East Coast Railway used to diverge. This route served neither Lancashire nor the east coast. A new bridge carries the Lincoln Relief Road across both the railway and the Fossdyke.

For much of the 6 miles to Saxilby the railway runs alongside this canal, which carried barges and pleasure boats. Passing under a 1930s bridge, the train then enters Saxilby Station. The present-day scene along the waterfront, with small shops, inns and residential housing crowded together, is very attractive, particularly in spring and summer when the bustle of boaters and anglers creates an animated picture. Some 3,000 people live here, a third of them working in Lincoln.

For the walker or cyclist there are two little gems of interest near here. Lovers of animals, particularly of horses, will find Bransby Horses' Rest Home worth a visit. The stables and pasture, about $2\frac{1}{4}$ miles from Saxilby, are home to over 100 animals, restored to good health after maltreatment by man. Many rescued animals were destined for the knacker's yard, either here or on the Continent, before being saved by the animal charity. A mile and a half north of Bransby is Stow, where St Mary's Church was seen earlier from the train. This is the mother-church of Lincoln Cathedral, the most monumental, impressive and important of pre-Conquest churches. The vast arches, over 30 feet high, on this limestone-built early eleventh-century building surpass in scale those of any other surviving Saxon church. Older parts of the church bear the scars of fires started during Viking raids.

As we leave Saxilby, we see on the east side of the track a loop for holding slow trains and next reach Sykes Junction, from where a disused branch leads to the River Trent at Torksey. Originally, this branch continued across the river to join the Gainsborough–Retford line at Clarborough.

A level-crossing and signal-box mark the site of the former Stow Park station, and the station house may be seen on the right. The goods on the east side is now a depot for Preston Farmers Limited. Here the railway crosses the Roman road, Till Bridge Lane, which ran from Lincoln (Lindum Colonia), home of a garrison of the Roman Ninth Legion, to the Great North Road. It was necessary to cross the River Trent by ford at Littleborough (Segelocum).

To the east, the ancient St Mary's Church, Stow, may be seen in the distance across the fields. The present church was commenced about 1050, on the site of an earlier fabric said to have been burnt by the Danes in 871.

Two miles further north is the site of the former Lea station in a deep cutting, spanned by several bridges carrying farm tracks. We bridge over Lea Road and enter Gainsborough's Lea Road Station. The town of Gainsborough is described on page 34.

The station is situated on an embankment and a curve, with staggered platforms. This was originally the terminal of a Great Northern Railway branch from Lincoln, opened in 1849. The station buildings, which are in the Italianate style or architecture favoured by the GNR, are at road level down two flights of stairs, and include the booking hall and booking office. The station is about one mile from the town centre, but town-service buses pass the door, and there are two taxi offices (one at the former station-master's house). North of the station is a goods-yard which is usually full of rail oil-tankers. Crude oil is extracted from many wells in and around Gainsborough and pumped by landlines to Gainsborough Lea Road goods-yard, where it is loaded into the oil-tankers. Generally two or three train-loads per week are sent out, *en route* to a refinery at Llandarcy.

Round a 90-degree curve to the left, the train joins the Barnetby line to cross the River Trent. Across the river is a further junction, with many trains veering south-west towards Retford and Sheffield, with the cooling towers of West Burton power station clearly visible.

The Doncaster route swings to the north, passing Beckingham – where the signal-box controls loop lines on either side of the tracks, and Walkeringham, before reaching Misterton, a large village where Newell Dunford's engineering works may be seen to the east, and where campaigning has begun for a station to serve this growing community.

Out into rich warp land, the train passes the site of Haxey for Epworth and Park Drain stations. Until 1933 you could catch an Axholme Joint Railway train from Haxey to John Wesley's birthplace at Epworth, and to Crowle and Goole.

Sprinter service leaves Lincoln Station. (*Photo*: Peter Cronin)

At the northern end of this flat stretch we see RAF Finningley to the west. This airfield is currently used by Dominie aircraft in the training of navigation officers, although its future is in some doubt because of mining subsidence between the runways. All the village stations between Doncaster and Gainsborough were gradually closed during the post-war period, the first being Finningley (7 miles), where the signal-box and platforms still remain. In recent years Finningley has received special passenger trains in connection with the annual air show at the RAF base. These have not used the original station but a specially constructed tubular and wooden platform to the west of it, on the down side only, close to the airfield perimeter. It is served by a shuttle service from Doncaster and some long-distance excursions. After the show the platform is taken down again until the following year.

Soon we speed past Black Carr Junction, up and over the East Coast Main Line, past the large freight yards and into Doncaster. Our journey on the former Great Northern and Great Eastern Joint Line – 'the Joint Line' in railway circles to this day – is at an end.

PETERBOROUGH–DONCASTER
(East Coast Main Line)
by Trevor Garrod

For many visitors to Lincolnshire and Nottinghamshire, the main line from London King's Cross to Edinburgh Waverley forms an important part of the journey. The route from London to Peterborough is covered in our companion volume, *East Anglia by Rail*, and north of Doncaster in *Yorkshire by Rail*, *North East by Rail* and *Scotland by Rail*.

Peterborough is $76\frac{1}{4}$ miles from London and enjoys at least one train an hour from the capital, the fastest taking just 47 minutes. To Grantham, the first station in Lincolnshire, the fastest trains from London take only 63 minutes, an average of almost 100 miles an hour. Similarly, you can be whisked down from Leeds, Newcastle or Edinburgh in air-conditioned comfort at up to 125 mph, and soon at 140 mph.

High speeds are nothing new to this railway, however. It was built as a trunk route in the mid-nineteenth century by the Great Northern Railway – a company whose very name evokes the confidence and ambition of the Victorians who promoted it. The tracks slice their way boldly up through the shires, swiftly conveying large numbers of people and countless tonnes of freight between the south and Yorkshire, the north-east and Scotland.

Since its opening in 1852 this route has had a distinguished history. It was the first in the country to operate dining cars, introduced between London and Leeds in 1879. Nine years later the Great Northern and its partners farther north, the North Eastern and the North British railways, established a record speed from London to Edinburgh of 6 hours 48 minutes – beating the rival companies on the west coast route.

In 1895 rivalry between these two main routes to Scotland resulted in further competition to see which could record the fastest run from London to Aberdeen. This time the west coast companies won, but on the east coast line a new record was set of 6 hours 18 minutes from King's Cross to Edinburgh.

The 1920s saw non-stop expresses introduced from London to Leeds, Harrogate and Newcastle; and then on 1 May 1928, the first non-stop run from London to Edinburgh by the now legendary locomotive 4772 *Flying Scotsman*. This was, at the time, the world record non-stop run.

More records were to be broken – the locomotive *Papyrus* reaching 108 mph down Stoke Bank in 1934, and 112 mph being scored the following year by the 'Silver Jubilee' streamlined train. It was on this stretch of line, in the county of Lincolnshire, that the world speed record for steam – unbeaten to this day – was set on 3 July 1938: the A4 locomotive *Mallard* ran down to Peterborough at up to 126 mph.

Diesel trains started appearing on the route in 1958 and the $393\frac{1}{2}$ miles to Edinburgh were being covered in 6 hours. After 1961 no more steam locomotives roared their way with expresses across the Lincolnshire countryside other than on occasional specials. For nearly two decades 3300 hp 'Deltic' locomotives held sway, to be succeeded in their turn in the late 1970s by the present InterCity 125s. These in turn are being replaced by new Mark IV coaches and Electra 25kv locomotives as part of the largest mainline electrification scheme of the decade, approved by government in 1984, financed from British Rail's own resources, and completed south of Doncaster a year ahead of schedule.

The modern station of Peterborough is, for visitors from the south and East Anglia, the gateway to Lincolnshire. Following the closure of Peterborough East station, all trains have used this one (formerly called Peterborough North), giving better cross-country connections. The station was reconstructed between 1972 and 1974, with modest functional buildings and four through platforms – which are arguably too small for the large numbers of passengers now using them. Just to the east of the station is the Great Northern Hotel, recently expanded, and the ultra-modern Queensgate Shopping Centre.

The city of Peterborough, with a population of just over 100,000 is well worth a visit – whether for shopping, viewing the ornate cathedral built in the twelfth and thirteenth centuries or enjoying the riverside walks and Nene Valley Park with its five-mile steam railway. Peterborough has expanded greatly since the late 1960s and several new estates – or 'townships' – can be seen as the train heads northwards.

Five straight, level steel tracks head in this direction out of the city – three belong to the main line, two to the Express route to Leicester. To the right are further freight sidings. New England Locomotive depot, on the northern outskirts of the city, closed in 1969. A glance eastwards now reveals landscaped new roads and cycleways.

Just over three miles north of Peterborough Station is Werrington Junction, where the line to Spalding and Lincoln veers off to the north-east. Two miles further on the Express route departs to the west, and the main line continues as four tracks. The flat fenland gradually starts to undulate and by Essendine, 8.2 miles from Peterborough, we are in limestone hill country.

We are now climbing the well-engineered bank down which *Mallard* set the world speed record and reach the summit at Stoke, just over 100 miles from King's Cross. The gradient – 1 in 178 at its steepest point – presents little problem to our train. As we speed past the attractive stone-built village of Little Bytham (11.5 miles from Peterborough) on the left, can you spot the pub with 'Mallard' on its sign?

Just before milepost 100 the quadruple tracks are reduced to two and soon we enter Stoke Tunnel. Emerging from it into the valley of the infant River Witham, we descend a gentle 1 in 200 gradient. The trackbed of the former iron ore branch to High Dyke can be spotted to the left, as can the Great North Road on the opposite side of the valley. Through gaps in the trees we see the attractive limestone village of Great Ponton before slowing for the approach to Grantham.

The handsome spire of St Wulfram's Church, one of many spires in this part of England, dominates this town of 28,000, which nestles between hills. St Wulfram's spire is 272 feet high and was in fact the tallest in England at the time when it was built at the end of the thirteenth century. Another remarkable feature of this church is its chained library, containing books dating back to 1472.

Grantham has a large market on Thursdays and Saturdays, and interesting old buildings in the town centre include two coaching inns, the George and the Angel & Royal. The latter dates from medieval times, and King John on occasion held court there. Grantham was an important place for changing horses on the Great North Road – and, from 1852 onwards, for changing steam locomotives on the Great Northern Railway.

The famous scientist Sir Isaac Newton was born nearby, and was educated at the town's grammar school, which still stands, in Church Street. A statue of Sir Isaac has been erected in the High Street, and his experiences with an apple are commemorated in the tastefully designed shopping centre named after him, adjacent to the new bus terminus and eight minutes' walk from the railway station. No statue has yet been erected to the other famous person hailing from these parts, Mrs Margaret Thatcher, but her birthplace in North Parade can still be seen.

Two nearby famous buildings well worth a visit are Belton House (3 miles north) and Belvoir (pronounced 'beevor') Castle (8 miles west). Both are within easy cycling distance; walkers can reach them via the Viking Way and Jubilee Way long-distance footpaths. For the less energetic, a weekday bus service to Lincoln passes Belton House (a National Trust property dating from the late seventeenth century). A less frequent bus service to Melton Mowbray can be used for part of the way to Belvoir Castle.

Grantham Station, which was tastefully rebuilt and modernized in the mid-1980s, is also the junction for the Skegness line and for the line that runs westwards across the Vale of Belvoir to Nottingham. Main line trains head north through the short Peascliffe Tunnel, past the junction at Barkston and over the direct line that enables trains from the Midlands to Skegness to avoid Grantham.

The high land is left behind us as we head north-west over flat farmland through the long-closed stations of Houghton and Claypole and across the Nottinghamshire border to Newark, 120 miles from King's Cross.

Newark-on-Trent (population 25,000) is an ancient and attractive market town well worth breaking your journey to visit. The town centre is ten minutes' walk from Northgate Station (on the main line) and five minutes from Castle Station on the Lincoln–Nottingham line.

The centre of the town is a large cobbled market square bordered by many buildings of note, including the beautifully restored fourteenth-century Old White Hart, the Governor's House and the Moot Hall. Close by is the magnificent parish church of St Mary Magdalene with its massive spire.

Nearby are the remains of the castle which, at the time of writing, are being restored. King John died here in 1216. To help visitors, the castle houses an interpretative centre, but it is not always open, although Wednesday afternoon invariably finds it staffed. A short walk along the River Trent from the castle is the Millgate Museum of Folk Life and the Millgate Conservation Area (telephone

Newark 78962 for tourist information).

Newark has hourly buses to the small town of Southwell, and it is worth trying to catch one whose route is via the pretty Trentside village of Fiskerton. Southwell is dominated by the Norman Minster, built between the twelfth and fourteenth centuries with twin towers and intricate carvings. Close to the Minster is the Saracen's Head, a seventeenth-century inn where Charles I gave himself up in 1646. Buses can also take you from Newark to the extensive collection of historic aircraft preserved at Winthorpe.

Newark has numerous restaurants and cafés and many pubs serve food. Real ale enthusiasts will not be disappointed and should look for pubs selling 'Home Ales' if they wish to sample a local beer. Bass, Ruddles and Marstons can also be had. To enjoy Newark at its best, try to visit it on a Wednesday, the traditional market day when the town is vibrant and bustling.

Back on the main line, our train crosses the Nottingham–Lincoln line on the level just north of Northgate Station, and immediately afterwards the River Trent. It then speeds due north for several miles, across low-lying land often flooded in winter, parallel to the Great North Road and the river, past Muskham (where in steam days there were water-troughs for locomotives to replenish their stocks while travelling), then veering north-west again, past the earthworks of the former Dukeries Junction, where the Lincoln–Chesterfield route crossed ours.

The city of Lincoln is 15 miles to the east at this point and its cathedral can be seen on a clear day. Rather nearer to the line we can see, from time to time, the cooling towers of power stations along the banks of the Trent.

Seven miles further on is Retford (population 18,000), whose large market place has many dignified buildings and a certain Flemish appearance. Three miles

Class 91 locomotive passes Newark Northgate Station on a north-bound test train. (*Photo*: P. Cronin)

north of the town is Lound Nature Reserve, which is passed by some of the Retford–Doncaster buses.

Retford Station, 138½ miles from King's Cross, is on two levels. We run in to the main line, high-level platforms and can change here for trains from the low-level platforms for Gainsborough and (less frequently) Kirton and Brigg; or for Worksop and Sheffield.

There are no more stations open for the next 17 miles – but we flash past Scrooby (home of the Pilgrim Fathers) and Bawtry (once intended to be the junction for Sheffield) before goods lines and collieries herald the approach to Doncaster. The famous racecourse is seen to the east and its most famous race, the St Leger, has given its name to the station buffet. (Railway gastronomes may also like to note that the 'Trax' fast-food restaurant on Doncaster Station was the first to be opened on BR.) Most trains stop at Doncaster, and as we draw into the station we can see the locomotive works to the west of the line. They were established here in 1853 and have contributed to the growth of this town of 82,000 people.

We are now 156 miles from King's Cross, in the home town of Edmund Denison, who was the driving force behind the building of this fast route to the north. The busy station, rebuilt in the 1940s, is the junction for routes to Sheffield, Leeds, Hull and Grimsby – a major centre on what British Rail calls the East Coast Main Line, or to use its more evocative earlier name, the Great Northern Railway.

NOTTINGHAM–GRANTHAM–SKEGNESS
by Robert Waite

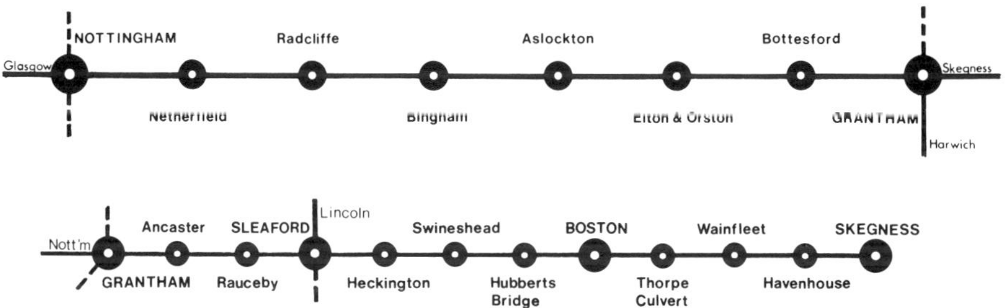

The first 2¾ miles out of Nottingham are shared with trains on the route to Lincoln as far as Netherfield Junction. Here the Grantham line, opened on 15 July 1850, heads south-west through Netherfield Station, over Rectory Junction, and past the new Victoria Park development on the site of Colwick marshalling yards, an ideal site to investigate for a possible new station. Trains cross the River Trent by a viaduct, after which a freight-only line, opened in 1960, leaves ours and curves south to Cotgrave Colliery. We then head east to Radcliffe-on-Trent, where a 100-foot high red cliff stands next to the river and overlooks the surrounding countryside.

Leaving Radcliffe we continue to head east across the fairly flat farmland into the Vale of Belvoir (pronounced 'beevor'). To the north lies Newton airfield. About halfway to Bingham was Saxondale Junction, where a line left ours and headed south-east to join the Newark–Bottesford–Market Harborough line near Harby. The Saxondale–Harby line closed to passengers on 7 December 1953 and to freight in 1962.

We then cross over the A46 by bridge. This road runs along part of the course of a Roman road called the Fosse Way between Lincoln and Exeter. About 1 mile north-east along the A46 is the site of a Roman settlement, Margidunum. This is said to have covered seven acres and was large enough for a garrison of 1,000 men. By the end of the first century it was no longer used as a military station, but continued as a town. Roman coins, pottery and other relics have been discovered on a site in this area.

Stone from the ramparts of Margidunum was used to construct the church tower at Bingham. The spire was added later and reaches 120 feet, dominating this little market town which has had several notable residents in its history.

The Rector here for many years was the father of Sir Christopher Wren, architect of St Paul's Cathedral. The actress Lily Langtry often stayed at the Rectory. The author James Prior Kirk moved to Bingham in 1891 and died there in 1922. Today Bingham is the home of Dennis McCarthy, the radio and television broadcaster.

Halfway between Bingham and Aslockton Station we cross from British Rail's Midland region into the Eastern region. Aslockton is the birthplace of Thomas Cranmer (1489–1556), later Archbishop Cranmer, advisor to Henry VIII during his break with the Church of Rome. The Cranmers' manor house, just north of the railway, has now gone. The present church was built in 1891 of Ancaster stone.

The railway crosses the River Smite $\frac{1}{2}$ mile east of Aslockton Station, and we next call at Elton & Orston Station which serves these two nearby villages. It was once hoped that Orston, $\frac{1}{2}$ mile north of the station, would develop into a spa resort, but this was not to be. The earliest part of its church dates from the thirteenth century. In a recess in the wall is placed a drum from the Battle of Waterloo.

Elton is $\frac{3}{4}$ mile south of the station. The church of St Michael and All Angels here is only 15 feet wide. In 1780 the verger dug up 200 silver pennies dating from Henry II's reign, from the churchyard. There was a similar incident at Orston, where 1,500 coins from the Civil War were unearthed in 1952.

Halfway between Elton & Orston and Bottesford stations, we cross from Nottinghamshire into the northernmost tip of Leicestershire and see the remains of the Newark–Market Harborough route, otherwise known as the Great Northern and London & North Western Joint Railway. The northern section of this from Newark closed to freight in 1988; the southern section in 1962.

Shortly after the junction we cross over the River Devon to Bottesford, the most northerly village in Leicestershire with the largest village church in the county. It also has the county's tallest spire, reaching 210 feet. There are memorials to eight Dukes of Rutland in the building.

On a clear day it is possible to see Belvoir Castle, situated on a hill overlooking the surrounding countryside, 3 miles south of the railway. The present castle is built on the site of a medieval fortress and has been extensively rebuilt during the seventeenth, eighteenth and nineteenth centuries. It has been the seat of the Dukes of Rutland since Henry VIII's time. The castle is open to the public and special events include medieval jousting tournaments.

The train heads eastwards, $1\frac{1}{2}$ miles beyond Bottesford passing Belvoir Junction where a freight-only line left ours and headed south to Denton. This was used by trains carrying ironstone until the branch closed in 1973.

Next comes the site of Sedgebrook Station, closed to passengers on 2 July 1956, and a mile further on Allington Junction, where the Grantham Avoiding Line, opened in 1875, curves away to our left. This is used by occasional freight trains, typically carrying imported steel from Boston docks to the Midlands, and by summer passenger trains to Skegness.

Our line heads south-west, under the Great North Road and through $\frac{1}{4}$-mile Gonerby Tunnel. Now the town of Grantham is ahead of us and soon we come to rest in its station. Notes on what to see in Grantham can be found on page 13.

Our train reverses at Grantham Station, where the bay platform (3) is generally used for departures to Skegness and the west platform (4) for departures to Nottingham.

Our train heads out 'under the wires' on the East Coast Main Line to Barkston South Junction, where we curve sharply eastwards on a single track (15 mph) to rejoin the Grantham line at Barkston East Junction. The crossover points at Barkston South Junction have been re-sited further south, so trains to Skegness now travel a longer distance on the 'wrong line' (up main) before taking the sharp curve to Barkston East.

We cross the River Witham and pass the old Harrington Station closed to passengers on 9 September 1962. East of the station was a junction where a line left ours and headed northwards to Leadenham, Waddington and Lincoln. The start of the trackbed of this route is still just visible, although it was closed to passengers and freight on 30 October 1965, except for a short section from Lincoln to Bracebridge Gas Works, which stayed open for freight until 1971. There was also an east-facing junction at Harrington, which only saw a short period of use, as it was abandoned on the opening of the 'Joint Line' in 1882, as the latter provided a quicker route from Lincoln to Sleaford.

Our train heads east, with hills on cither side, over Sudbrooke level-crossing,

Statue of Sir Isaac Newton
at Grantham.
(*Photo*: Peter Cronin)

Sprinter near Heckington. (*Photo*: John C. Baker)

through another cutting, past the remains of lime kilns, and into Ancaster Station. Ancaster was a Roman town called Causennae, and is sited on Ermine Street, a Roman road. Much has been found from Causennae, including coins and mosaic pavements. Near the station are maltings which opened in 1857.

We leave Ancaster on an embankment, cross the River Slea twice and pass through a cutting. Approaching Wilsford level-crossing we have an aerial view of Wilsford village on our right from a second embankment. Passing Wilsford Warren golf course (the home of Sleaford Golf Club) we cross the River Slea for the third and fourth time before arriving at Rauceby Station. Much use is made of this small station by patients, staff and visitors travelling to and from the nearby psychiatric hospital, the boiler-house chimney of which is just visible above the trees in the extensive wooded grounds.

We head north-east through a cutting and pass the small village of Quarrington to the south-east, before curving eastwards and passing over the site of a junction where a small branch line left ours and ran northwards to RAF Cranwell between 1919 and August 1956. This branch had an intermediate station called Slea River and several gradients, the steepest being 1 in 50.

At Sleaford West Junction where the trackwork and signalling were modernised four years ago, 'Joint Line' traffic from Lincoln joins us and we pull into Sleaford Station, where connections can also be made for Spalding and Peterborough. The town of Sleaford is described in the Peterborough–Lincoln section on pages 6–8.

The route from Sleaford to Boston was opened on 13 April 1859 and first passes the maltings. This section of line has been singled, and we pass the junction with the Peterborough line, and then run under the Sleaford avoiding line. Passing Kirkby Laythorpe we head out across fairly flat country to Heckington, where the station also serves the village of Great Hale.

Heckington Station buildings were taken over and restored by Heckington Village Trust in 1976 and are used by them as offices and meeting rooms. Adjacent to the station entrance is the Pea Room, a red-brick warehouse which was built for processing peas. It is now in the hands of the Village Trust, and is used as a craft centre and tourist information office. The only eight-sailed windmill in England overlooks the station. Built in 1830, its tower reaches 55 feet, and the milling equipment is maintained in full working order. It is open to the public at certain times for demonstrations – details can be obtained from the Pea Room information centre. Also worth a visit is Heckington's fine fourteenth-century church, whose 182-foot spire, like the unique windmill, is a local landmark.

Beyond Heckington the route becomes double track again and we cross the Great Fen, passing over the two Great Hale level-crossings. Soon the Forty Foot Drain joins us on the south, and we run side by side until Boston. Crossing the A17 road we arrive at Swineshead Station, popular with fishermen in the summer months. On the right-hand side of the station is a new and eye-catching addition to the Plough Inn. It is a vintage ex-GNR coach, used for many years as a stores van in the sidings as Boston Station, now beautifully restored in original teak livery and shortly to be used as a restaurant. The centre of Swineshead village lies 2 miles south-east. King John stayed at the abbey near here, a fact mentioned in Shakespeare's *King John*.

Leaving Swineshead, the line is now 'sandwiched' between the Drain and the main road to Boston. Crossing more fenland, our train arrives at Hubberts Bridge Station, named after Hubba the Dane. This is another useful station for fishermen, and the adjacent bridge carries the B1192 road, replacing an earlier structure which carried a turnpike. Also adjacent to the station is an old wharf and a large warehouse, now used by a well-known fertilizer company.

The line returns to single track at this point and soon we see Boston airfield on the north side, used mainly by crop-spraying aircraft. To the south of the Drain lies Boston Sports Stadium, a well-known venue for national speedway fans.

Passing over Wyberton level-crossing, there is new housing on the north side and the line curves quite sharply northwards and we see Boston goods-yard to our right. This has recently been completely remodelled and two new sidings with road access installed. The remaining sidings are used as storage for freight traffic to and from the docks branch, which is now worked as far as the British Rail junction by Dock Authority personnel. The swing bridge leading to the docks branch was also modernised a few years ago and can now take large modern air-braked freight wagons. Freight traffic to and from the docks is somewhat intermittent, consisting mostly of steel, telegraph poles and continental produce, together with occasional grain shipments. There are hopes for further development of freight traffic to and from the docks when privatised.

On the western side we pass the remains of Broadfield Lane locomotive depot and over the level-crossing the Civil Engineers' workshops built by the Great Northern Railway in the 1890s and now occupied by the East Midlands Electricity Board. As we proceed over West Street level-crossing, the Trinity Street Feather Factory may be seen towards the east with a large swan emblem on the roof. This is the last surviving nineteenth-century building of this industry, built in 1877 for the purifying of feathers to be used in pillows and other products.

Boston Station has undergone much rationalisation over the years. Particularly noticeable is the large gap between the two platforms, now occupied by flower beds and pots. Here there were originally two 'through' running lines, but these were removed with the closure of the East Lincolnshire line. The history of railways in Boston is an interesting one, and has been dealt with at length in *The Railways of Boston* by N. R. Wright (History of Boston series), and also in two recently published books (*Boston – A Railway Town*, parts 1 and 2) by local author and travel agent Stephen Walker. Lines from Peterborough, Lincoln and Grimsby reached the town in 1848 and Boston was the headquarters of the Great Northern Railway's chief mechanical engineer from 1848 to 1852, when the plant was moved to Doncaster.

The town of Boston is dominated by the 272-foot-high tower of St Botolph's Church, a landmark for many miles around. 'Boston Stump', as it is popularly known, is one of the most famous churches in Lincolnshire, and displays a Flemish influence. Other interesting buildings include the Blackfriars' Hall, the eighteenth-century Fydell House, and the medieval Guildhall, now the town's museum.

It was from Boston that the Pilgrim Fathers made an unsuccessful attempt to sail across the Wash and North Sea for Holland. The cells in which they were imprisoned still remain. As well as being an ancient port, Boston is also a market town on Wednesdays and Saturdays.

We leave Boston Station heading north, on single track once again, and cross the River Witham by the most impressive of the bridges along the route, known as the Grand Sluice. The present iron bridge dates from 1885 and replaced an earlier wooden structure. The Grand Sluice itself was built in 1764–6 to improve drainage of the fens above Boston. Proceeding slowly round the reverse curves (20 mph and 30 mph) we pass over Horncastle Road level-crossing. Curving north-east into open countryside, we are now on what was the second longest stretch of straight line in Great Britain, on the former East Lincolnshire line from Boston to Burgh-le-Marsh. Picking up speed we pass over the Maud Foster Drain and several level-crossings in quick succession, and then cross the Cowbridge Drain, where Boston Golf Club's course can be seen on the left-hand side. At Sibsey our train slows down to 15 mph for a junction where we revert to double track, and pass Sibsey station which closed to passengers on 11 September 1961. There is local interest in reopening this station. Sibsey windmill, known as the Trader Mill and built in 1877, has been restored and is open to the public at certain times.

Travelling at speed again, we cross over the Hobhole Drain and can see, $1\frac{1}{4}$ miles north along it, the impressive Lade Bank pumping-station, built in 1877 with steam pumps, but operated by diesel pumps since 1940. We pass the remains of Old Leake Station closed to passengers on 17 September 1956, but still boasting an ex-Great Northern Railway somersault signal, where the signal arm is pivoted centrally instead of at the end. Other fine examples of these unusual signals can be found at Thorpe Culvert, Wainfleet and Havenhouse.

After crossing Spilsby Road we pass through Eastville Station, closed in 1961. Next we pass Bellwater Junction signal-box from where a direct line, closed from 5 October 1970, left ours for Woodhall Junction and Lincoln. Nothing can now be seen of the former trackbed of this line as it has now returned to being part of the adjacent farmland. As we pass Little Steeping Station, closed in 1961, the Lincolnshire Wolds can be seen in the distance on our left.

Soon after crossing the Steeping River we slow down to 15 mph for the Firsby South curve, which leads us to the Skegness branch proper, which was opened as far as Wainfleet to goods from 11 September 1871, to passengers from 24 October 1871, and opened to Skegness on 28 July 1873. Until the closure of the East Lincolnshire main line (to Grimsby) on 5 October 1970, Firsby was the junction station for the Skegness branch, where passengers were required to change trains on most occasions. The station was an impressive building with three platforms and an overall roof together with a unique arrangement of six overlapping level-crossing gates. Today all that remains is part of the station-master's house (still occupied by a local BR employee, who now works at Skegness Station) and the original GNR goods-shed. Part of this has been painted bright yellow and is now used by a local potato firm, and it can be seen from our train. Today virtually nothing can be seen of the former trackbed to Firsby Station or the former Spilsby branch – it has all now returned to fields.

As our train leaves the Firsby curve, it is interesting to note that this part of the track was not added until 1881, and was constructed as a diversion route for holiday trains from the Midlands, so they did not have to reverse at Firsby Station. This section of track was virtually disused throughout the winter months every year, with the South Junction signal box normally only being manned at weekends in the summer.

Picking up speed again we head south-east, over Lymn Bank level-crossing and reach Thorpe Culvert Station which, being close to the River Steeping, is popular with fishermen. The station buildings here were repaired and repainted in 1986.

The village of Thorpe St Peter, with its medieval church, is $\frac{3}{4}$ mile east of the station. Leaving the station we cross the Wainfleet Haven 'New Cut', pass over Brewster Lane and Matt Pitts Lane level-crossings and heading across Wainfleet Common (where the railway cut through a Danish barrow which was found to contain several graves) we arrive at Wainfleet Station, with flower beds carefully tended by the local Women's Institute. This well-used station serves the small town of Wainfleet All Saints, thought to be on or near the site of a Roman city called Vannona. Hopes that Wainfleet would develop into a major port came to nothing, as Boston took away its potential importance. In earlier years, however, the station did see extensive goods traffic. The site of the former goods-yard is now privately owned, although the original goods-shed does still survive, albeit looking rather worse for wear now. On the river bank beyond the goods yard site can be seen Salem Bridge Brewery, the last independent brewery in Lincolnshire, founded by George Bateman in 1874.

William of Waynflete, born in this town towards the end of the fourteenth century, became a famous bishop and Lord Chancellor of England. He founded Magdalen College, Oxford, and Wainfleet's own Magdalen College School, whose distinctive tall octagonal towers we can see on the left just after leaving the station. This school now serves as the town library. The line curves sharply to the left at this point (15 mph) and heading north-west we pass Chain Bridge level-crossing, and once again cross over the Wainfleet Haven 'New Cut', shortly before arriving at the remote Havenhouse Station, originally named Croft Bank and also popular with fishermen during the summer. This station featured several years ago in the BBC television series *Nanny* and was suitably repainted for the occasion. The station buildings have also been repaired and for a little-used station it presents a very fine appearance, enhanced by two Great Northern somersault signals which protect the level-crossing gates.

Continuing the final part of our journey over gentle reverse curves through Crofts Marsh, we pass the site of Seacroft Station, closed to passengers on 7 December 1953. Only the signal-box survives, but there are no signals. The town of Skegness now comes into view and the large amount of unoccupied land on either side of the line was at one time used as carriage sidings. Originally there

Boston Stump.
(*Photo:* Peter Cronin)

Skegness beach. (*Photo:* East Lindsey District Council)

were 12 on each side, but now only three remain on the left-hand side, these being used during the summer months for running-round and stabling locomotive-hauled trains.

The terminus station at Skegness has at present six platforms, only two of which are used regularly during the winter months. When the railway first reached the town in 1873, Skegness was a village of some 350 inhabitants. The town today is expanding quite considerably with a population approaching 15,000. Excursion trains to the resort have always been extremely popular: in 1882, 22,000 trippers visited what was then a new town, and the last train departed at 2.30 a.m., with some people still being left behind! The popularity of Skegness was boosted when the GNR commissioned John Hassall to draw a picture in 1908. This became a poster, showing a fisherman bounding over the golden sands with the slogan 'Skegness is so bracing'. This 'Jolly Fisherman' emblem continues to be the main feature of advertising for the resort today.

In 1977, BR introduced an economy measure to save on the wages of signalmen and crossing-keepers, opening the Boston–Skegness section of the line for only ten hours each day. Early morning and late evening trains were replaced by 'limited stop' buses, connecting with trains at Boston. As usually happens, these replacement buses were not popular with passengers and some years later were withdrawn. However, from May 1989, the Boston–Skegness section of line has reverted to two-shift operation restoring early morning and late evening trains. This was made possible by a seven-year project, jointly financed by British Rail and Lincolnshire County Council, to automate most of the level-crossings on the branch.

Other aspects of modernisation are also evident on the line. Most of the permanent speed restrictions have now been equipped with large new number signs, incorporating advanced warning boards linked into the audible warning system. Large aerials have been erected at Boston and adjacent to the signal-box at Skegness Station, to enable train drivers to be in direct radio contact with the signalmen at the few signal-boxes which remain in use.

Until 1988, Skegness Station had remained little altered from when it was built, but early in the year over half of the canopy over Platforms 3 and 4 was removed, and the remaining section now covers only about $2\frac{1}{2}$ coaches' length. The old waiting rooms have become a modern ticket and parcels office and waiting area. The ladies' toilets were also modernised. The new 'open plan' ticket and information office is very impressive and has brought Skegness Station up to date whilst maintaining the character of the original buildings. The Station Chef buffet, re-opened in 1987, is well patronised during the summer periods.

Skegness Station is a good transport interchange. The bus station conveniently adjoins the rail station, with regular bus services to Funcoast World (Butlins), Ingoldmells, Chapel St Leonards, Sutton-on-Sea and Mablethorpe. The beach is approximately 10 minutes' walk from the station through the town centre. Shopping in the town has recently been much improved with the opening of the new Hildreds Shopping Centre, at the top of High Street, and opposite the Co-op. The town has all the other amenities of a good seaside resort, including a childrens' indoor centre (Panda's Palace) and a new indoor swimming pool. There is also the traditional funfair, and the well-known Embassy Centre, which serves as a theatre and a conference and exhibition centre.

And there are further train rides to be enjoyed! Apart from two ghost-train rides on the seafront, there is a $\frac{1}{4}$-mile-long miniature railway between Tower Esplanade and Princess Parade; and three miles north at Funcoast World (formerly Butlins Holiday Camp, opened in 1937) there is a monorail, and an indoor water sports centre with modern water chutes and splash pools.

HUMBERLINK

By Mick Savage

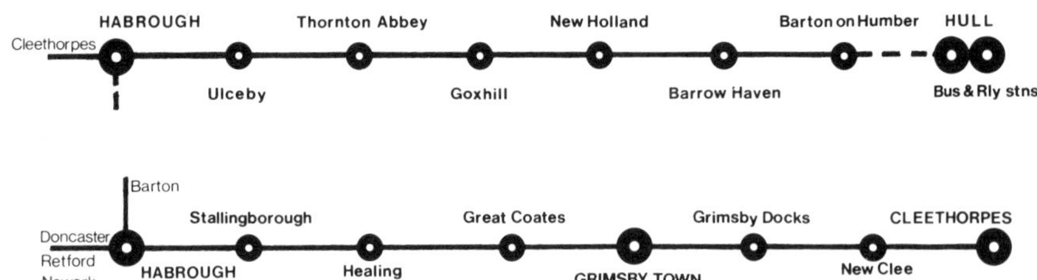

Humberlink is the brand name for the public transport service connecting the two major population centres of the county of Humberside – Hull and Grimsby/Cleethorpes – via the Humber Bridge. The facility consists of a bus service from Hull bus station (adjacent to the railway station) to Barton on Humber interchange (bus and rail station combined), from where the journey is continued by train to Grimsby and Cleethorpes. At the time of writing (May 1989) through ticketing is NOT available. You pay for the bus on the bus; and for the train at manned stations (i.e. Habrough, Grimsby Town and Cleethorpes), or if you join at an unmanned station, on the train.

Unfortunately, the bus service cannot accommodate cycles or prams, but it is possible (and very rewarding on a nice day!) to cycle or walk over the Humber Bridge free of charge, having arrived at or intending to depart from Barton by train. It is about eight miles from Barton interchange to the centre of Hull, so those pushing prams beware!

Now the largest centre of population on the east coast between Tyneside and London, with around 260,000 residents, Hull grew up where the River Hull flows into the Humber and became a great seaport. Its correct name is Kingston upon Hull, but over the course of time the 'Kingston upon' has been dropped.

Hull is a pleasant city, not at all the mental image that many will conjure up. There is an excellent range of shops, with all the well-known stores, close to the station, and a market in the Old Town about a mile out of the centre. The bus station is just off Ferensway, next to Paragon Railway Station, which is handy for making rail connections to or from the Bridlington and Scarborough line.

The bus to look for is the 350 service for Scunthorpe, which calls at Barton interchange *en route*. Humberlink is based on an hourly frequency during the day, but with only one evening departure, the journey time to Barton being about 25 minutes. Buses are provided by East Yorkshire and Roadcar. There are less frequent Sunday services.

On leaving Hull bus station the route taken passes the Infirmary ($\frac{3}{4}$ mile) and the entrance to West Park ($1\frac{1}{4}$ miles), both on the right. Also on the right is the large Pickering Park with many leisure facilities (2 miles), and then on the left is Boothferry Park, the home of Hull City Football Club ($2\frac{1}{2}$ miles).

Very soon the towers of the Humber Bridge appear on the left, and in no time we are on its approach road. At this point, sit back and admire this magnificent structure, the longest single-span suspension bridge in the world. Its main span is 4626 feet, 366 feet longer than the span of the bridge over the Verrazano Narrows in New York. The Humber Bridge provides two dual-lane carriageways with separate footpaths/cycleways on each side, and the bridge clears high water by 98 feet.

Without doubt the best way to see the bridge is by walking or cycling over it. Walking takes about 30 minutes, the distance being some 1½ miles. There are refreshments and toilets at a car and coach park on the north bank, and also at the viewing area in Barton. Refreshments are available most of the year at weekends but only in summer during the week. On a clear night the bridge is an awe-inspiring sight, with lights twinkling into the distance. The high ground of the Yorkshire Wolds and Lincolnshire Wolds provides a magnificent backdrop.

The bus continues past the toll booths and up onto the bridge itself. Now the enormity of the undertaking hits you. Look left, back to Hull, and Barton on the south bank. Look right, up-river towards Goole and Selby. Seagoing vessels, most fairly small, pass under the bridge *en route* for the Trent wharves, Goole or Selby, or alternatively Rotterdam or Antwerp. All too soon we are over the bridge and the bus winds its way down to Barton, to the railway station where an interchange was built in 1981. Here we leave the bus and walk across to the diesel railcar waiting in the single platform. Cleethorpes is 23 miles (50 minutes) away, and Grimsby Town 20 miles (40 minutes).

If we are continuing our journey immediately, the train will be away in three or four minutes. But why not have a quick look at Barton, a small town with 8,000 inhabitants?

The town grew up around Barton Haven, a few hundred yards on the riverward side of the station. The first passenger ferry from the south to the north bank of the Humber commenced in 1832 from Barton Haven to Hull, but transferred to New Holland (four miles to the east) from 1848 with the coming of the railway to that village, and the building of its pier. If you want to find out more, walk from the station up Fleetgate as far as it goes, then left on Holydyke for 300 yards

Humber Bridge. (*Photo:* Peter Cronin)

to the library, where tourist information is obtainable (or telephone Barton 32245).

There are two historic churches in the old part of the town, reached through the narrow streets, and also a large park (Baysgarth Park) with sports facilities and an indoor swimming pool open to the public. Hostelries abound, three worthy of mention being the Coach and Horses, High Street; The Sloop, Waterside Road; and the Wheatsheaf, Holydyke. All are around seven minutes walk from the station.

We now join the train for the journey to Cleethorpes. We shall travel through flat but pleasantly pastoral countryside, part of the Lincolnshire marshes, a strip of land down the coast reclaimed from the sea hundreds of years ago.

The line out of Barton is straight for over three miles. Between railway and river to the left are Barton Broads, a series of lakes popular with anglers. Weekly fishing holidays with caravans on site, or daily fishing tickets can be purchased. Look back through the trees for another view of the Humber Bridge; look across the river to the Hull waterfront.

Just before Barrow Haven Station (a request halt) are further lakes (old clay pits), the home of Barton Sailing Club and Barton Water Ski Club. Only 2–3 minutes' walk inland along the narrow road is the Haven Inn, whose public bars and restaurant are very popular with the locals. Walk back again and over the railway, to have a look at the haven itself. Your view will be different depending on the state of the tide; boats either bobbing around or stuck deep in silt. By crossing the haven by the old railway bridge, you can reach the sailing and water ski clubs. Follow the path round past the club houses and along the Humber bank, with breathtaking views of the Humber Bridge and Hull (don't forget your binoculars), for a 2-mile walk back into Barton.

Our train continues past more water-filled clay pits before reaching New Holland. As the track curves here, look left at the rail-served grain terminal. Here until June 1981, but now gone completely, was New Holland Town Station, leading on to the pier and the pier station, from where paddle-steamers sailed for Hull Corporation pier. Now the grain-exporting ships have taken their place.

We arrive at the New Holland halt built by Humberside County Council in 1981, and once again there is a popular hostelry close at hand. The Lincoln Castle Hotel is a free house and is named after one of the class of three 'Castle' steam-driven paddle-steamers used on the New Holland–Hull service into the late 1970s.

Leaving New Holland our train gives up the single line token at Oxmarsh Crossing signal-box and joins a double-track section of line. Now heading inland we see on both sides of the line arable land stretching as far as the eye can see. A sense of loneliness prevails, with very few houses in sight and fields stretching to the horizon. Then, suddenly, we reach Goxhill Station, 4 minutes out of New Holland and 14 from Barton. The quiet village is dominated by the handsome parish church of All Saints, while $\frac{1}{2}$ mile to the east are the picturesque remains of a priory incorporated into a farmhouse.

From Goxhill the scenery remains pleasant, and in a few minutes the tree-framed ruins of Thornton Abbey are sighted on the left, $\frac{1}{4}$ mile from the railway. Thornton Abbey Station is a request stop, and a bridle-way leads across a field from the station straight to the fourteenth-century gatehouse. The abbey is in the care of English Heritage. The gardens are open all year, but the abbey gatehouse is open on weekends only from November to March 10 a.m.–4 p.m., and from Wednesday to Sunday from April to October 10 a.m.–6 p.m. There is a small admission charge, currently 80p for adults with reductions for children, O.A.P.s etc. Telephone Killingholme 40357 for details. Thornton Curtis village, with its interesting parish church, is a pleasant 2-mile walk or cycle ride to the west. The road is signposted from Thornton Abbey Station.

South of the station, strange-shaped buildings can be seen on the left. These are the two oil refineries only a couple of miles away at Killingholme. They are a rare sight at night, a whole mass of lights. We soon reach the junction station of Ulceby, where oil trains use the tracks which trail in on the left, and we cross over to the one remaining platform. Actually this is Ulceby Skitter – the village of Ulceby is over a mile away. Once again there is a public house close by the station, if you want to stay a while or maybe start or finish your own walk or cycle ride here.

On leaving Ulceby our train curves round to the left on a single line through a small area of woodland and under the A180 trunk road. Soon the main railway line into Grimsby appears on the right, and we join it before running into Habrough Station. Once again close at hand is a popular watering-hole, the Station Hotel, recently refurbished.

Habrough is the railhead for Immingham, population 15,000, a port two miles to the east, well known for its bulk cargoes of oil and iron ore. Immingham has a new museum in Waterworks Street, open Tuesdays to Sundays 10 a.m.–4 p.m., other times by appointment. Telephone Immingham 75777 for details. Admission is free. St Andrews Church is worth a visit, and opposite it is a memorial to the Pilgrim Fathers, who sailed from Immingham to Holland in 1609.

After Habrough the line again cuts through rich farmlands and cuts across the former Immingham–Grimsby main road at Little London crossing. Half a mile further on to the right can be seen a delightful church apparently in the middle of a field miles from anywhere. This is Stallingborough's parish church of St Peter and St Paul.

Our train soon calls at Stallingborough, Healing and Great Coates Stations in quick succession. These villages all owe their expansion to the coming of the railway in 1848. A couple of minutes after leaving Great Coates the Grimsby Leisure Centre is passed on the right. Here you can indulge in indoor bowls, ice-skating, squash, roller-skating, badminton, or swimming in the fun pool. The centre is open daily 9 a.m.–11 p.m.

We now enter the built-up area of central Grimsby, and as the train slows to not much more than walking pace we pass the beautiful St James Church, Grimsby's parish church, on the left, and then, about 40 minutes after leaving Barton, we slip quietly under the overall roof of the rather quaint Grimsby Town Station.

The line onwards to Cleethorpes has recently been singled, and passes through a continuous built-up area, but there are still surprises in store. A couple of minutes out of Grimsby Town, as the train approaches Grimsby Docks Station the seemingly pencil-thin Dock Tower can be seen straight ahead. It was built to house the hydraulic machinery necessary to work the gates to the Royal Dock when this was first constructed.

After Grimsby Docks Station the train passes close to the Royal Dock, on the left, and then negotiates a very sharp reverse curve. Look to the left again whilst on this curve and you will get a glimpse of the Fish Dock.

New Clee is the next station, and just after it the train crosses from Grimsby into Cleethorpes. In a few seconds we pass the home of Grimsby Town Football Club, Blundell Park, on the right. It is said that Grimsby Town play all their matches away from home, because the ground is actually in Cleethorpes! Almost immediately we are on the narrowest section of the sea wall. In 1978 the sea inundated the land behind this section of wall, as a result of which the present sea wall was built. We now slow down past the old Wonderland (now a market hall) and many amusement arcades on the left and enter Cleethorpes Station. Not many seaside resorts can boast a railway station actually on the promenade!

Grimsby and Cleethorpes may not be blessed with the tourist attractions of Lincoln or York, but there are still plenty of interesting things to see and do. Within 1½ miles (30 minutes' walk) of Grimsby Town Station can be found St James Parish Church in St James Square; People's Park in Welholme Road; Welholme Galleries (a museum of local history open Tuesday–Saturday 10 a.m.–5 p.m., admission free) in Welholme Road; Grimsby Leisure Centre in Cromwell Road; Scartho Swimming Baths in Scartho Road; Cannon Cinema (3 screens) in Freeman Street; an indoor market in Bull Ring Lane and another in Freeman Street (both in full swing on Tuesdays, Fridays and Saturdays).

A new attraction in Grimsby is the 'Iron Age Settlement'. This has been built in Weelsby Avenue, about 1½ miles from the town centre. The idea is to portray the buildings and people as they would have looked in the Iron Age. This 'interpretive centre' will be open April to September, Monday to Friday only 10 a.m.–4 p.m., admission free. Our further attraction accessible from Grimsby is Waltham windmill. Walk out of Grimsby Town Station to the main road and turn left. Here you will find the 9S and 9X bus stop. Take the bus to the terminus in Waltham and walk for a further 3–4 minutes along Brigsley Road to the preserved windmill which is open most Sunday afternoons, with occasional working days (weather permitting).

For current details of all these and other attractions, contact the Tourist Information Centre on Grimsby 240410. Recommended hostelries are: The Wheatsheaf (Bargate, 10 minutes), County Hotel (Brighowgate, 2 minutes), Royal Oak (Victoria Street, 7 minutes) and Yarborough Hotel directly outside the station. The privately-owned buffet on the station serves hot snacks and all-day breakfasts and is good value for money. It is open 6 a.m.–5.30 p.m. Monday to Saturday.

Cleethorpes is a completely separate town, although the boundary is only an imaginary line down the middle of Park Street. Attractions within a short walk of the station are: North Promenade and Wonderland (amusements and Sunday Market); Cleethorpes Leisure Centre (swimming pool, badminton, squash etc.); miniature railway and boating lake off Kings Road; gardens all along the seafront; Wednesday Market (outdoor) in Market Street; Old Clee Church in Clee Crescent. Also off Kings Road a new ten pin bowling alley has opened.

Of the many catering places close at hand, mention must be made of Steels Corner House, nationally known for the excellence of its fried fish meals. There are other meals on the menu as well, and the opening hours are 11.45 a.m.–10.30 p.m. seven days a week. Steels is in Market Street, only three minutes from the station. Another good class fish and chip restaurant should be open in 1989 immediately outside the station (turn left) in the old station tea room.

Only a bus ride away are the miniature golf course, Beacholme Holiday Camp and Beacholme Sunday Market – a massive summer Sunday Market at the holiday camp. Join the 9S or 9X bus at Sea road (1 minute from station) – the destination blind should show North Sea Lane. These buses will also take you to the leisure centre, bowling alley, miniature railway and boating lake if you don't feel like walking! For tourist information, telephone Cleethorpes 200220.

Finally, a couple of ideas for walkers and cyclists. This is ideal country for both, as there are few hills, and the secondary roads are very quiet.

The cyclist may alight at Barrow Haven and, after exploring the haven, set off down the road towards Barrow on Humber. This village is a conservation area with interesting buildings and churches deserving closer inspection.

From Barrow follow the A1077, signposted Grimsby, for 2½ miles to the pretty village of Thornton Curtis. One again, the church is worth a visit. A mile further on is Wootton, its houses and church grouped pleasantly round a large village pond with ducks and swans.

From Wootton village, return to the B1211, signposted Ulceby and Grimsby, from where it is another mile of pleasant scenery to Ulceby village, with its handsome church and pleasant pubs. Turn left onto the A160 towards Immingham and continue through Ulceby village to Ulceby Station (over a mile past the village). This pleasant, easy ride of about seven miles makes a relaxing morning or afternoon.

For the walker, how about alighting at Thornton Abbey Station, visiting the abbey ruins and then returning to the road crossed on the walk from the station? Turn left here and continue for $\frac{3}{4}$ mile, then bear right and over the railway line. The road then turns sharp left and continues parallel with the railway for 2 miles until meeting the A160. Turn left, and follow A160 for $\frac{1}{4}$ mile to Ulceby Station. You are unlikely to meet many cars on this three-mile stroll through a quiet rural area which is nevertheless within easy reach of the main centres of Hull and Grimsby.

DONCASTER–SCUNTHORPE–CLEETHORPES

by Brian J. Hastings

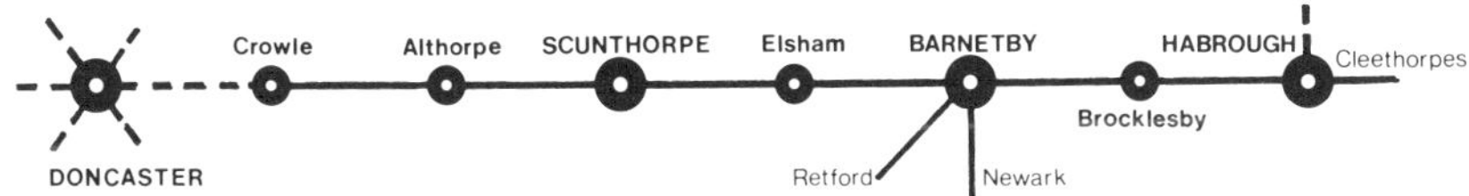

Of all the routes serving the historical county of Lincolnshire, and since 1974 the emergent county of Humberside, the line from Doncaster to Cleethorpes (described in this chapter as far as Habrough) offers probably the greatest contrast in scenery, land use and settlement.

Doncaster, only 98 minutes away from London by InterCity 125, is an important engineering centre, a South Yorkshire market town and railway junction on the East Coast Main Line. The station is very conveniently placed for access to the town's Arndale and Waterdale shopping centres and markets, and our train journey normally commences at Platforms 4, 6 or 7.

We part company with the main line just north of the Don bridge at Marshgate Junction and swing off north-eastwards following the Don flood plain, crossing the river and the South Yorkshire Canal, recently modernised, at Kirk Sandall, where South Yorkshire Passenger Transport Authority is opening a new station. The industrial nature of South Yorkshire is still apparent here, with the Volkswagen car preparation centre and the rail-served Rockware Glass plant. Little sign exists of Barnby Dun Station, closed in 1965, and we press on across the rich brown soil of the Bunter sandstone to Stainforth and Hatfield (7 miles out of Doncaster). This station serves the historic village of Hatfield plus the colliery villages of Stainforth, Dunscroft and Dunsville. It was reconstructed in 1978 during track-work realignment occasioned by the Doncaster area resignalling. Hatfield Main Colliery, on our left, marks the eastern limit of the South Yorkshire coalfield at the present time, although with severe flooding problems it is not now in production.

After passing beneath the M180 motorway at Thorne Junction, the line to Hull parts company on our left and we skirt the southern edge of Thorne, a historic market town expanded by the opening of Thorne Colliery in 1926. The pit has

Wootton, with its village pond, is a pleasant stopping place in South Humberside. (*Photo:* Trevor Garrod)

suffered severe flooding problems but is due to reopen in the future; the modern pit-gear towers can be seen to the north. Our step is at Thorne South (10 miles), which is convenient for the nearby South Common housing estate, to which there is footpath access.

The route now keeps company with the Stainforth–Keadby branch of the South Yorkshire Canal and for some eight miles we run along the canal bank on our right. It is an interesting reminder that this section of railway was built by the South Yorkshire Canal Company on its own towpath, needing no Act of Parliament and providing a clear case of 'if you can't beat them, then join them' (the Canal Company needing to protect its coal-carrying interests).

The scenery is now completely flat but not without interest. To the left lies the vast acreage of Thorne and Crowle Waste, a naturalists' paradise of peat bog and birch scrub; to the right are the fertile levels of the Isle of Axholme wrung from the swamp in 1626 by the efforts of the Dutch drainage engineer Cornelius Vermuyden. Settlements hereabouts are few and far between, and the stations at Maud's Bridge, Medge Hall and Godnow Bridge have all long since closed; but soon we are at Crowle (16 miles), one of the Isle of Axholme's leading settlements. The station lies just beyond an imposing fly-over viaduct carrying the A161 road over the line and canal.

Crowle Station serves the village of Ealand and the town of Crowle, and acts as a convenient railhead for many Isle of Axholme villages, notably Epworth with its Wesley connections, including the rectory much visited by Methodists from all over the world. Cyclists wishing to explore the area find Crowle Station a convenient railhead for their tours and fishermen, trying their skill in the canal or many local drains, also alight here.

The short run to the Trentside settlement of Keadby follows, with the closed Keadby power-station standing silent on our left. At Keadby we cross the canal for the last time and climb by way of an embankment to Althorpe ($19\frac{1}{2}$ miles), a station serving Althorpe and Keadby villages, and which lies alongside the A18 road. Connection with local buses can be made for journeys to Belton or Epworth.

Ahead lies the King George V Bridge taking us and the road over the tidal Trent. There are views of the busy Trentside wharves and shipping passing beneath. The bridge, opened in 1916, has a lifting mechanism but became 'fixed' in 1958. Signs on the right of old abutments and some disused track remind us that an earlier bridge existed here from 1864 to 1916, this being a rail-only swing structure replaced by the one we have just used.

Descent from the bridge embankment to the Trent flood plain is a brief prelude to a steep ascent at 1 in 93 to breast the prominent wooded escarpment we can see ahead. The climb begins on a viaduct which once boasted 29 arches, then continues on a steep embankment and is completed within a deep cutting to reach Scunthorpe (23 miles).

The town owes its origins to the local discovery of iron ore in 1859, which in turn led to iron- and steel-making becoming the principal industry. Despite its music hall image, Scunthorpe is a pleasant, clean and spacious town with many amenities. Normanby Hall and Country Park is about three miles north and easily reached by bus. The station itself is close to the borough museum, the attractive old Church of St Lawrence and the Civic Theatre.

Our journey for the next two miles threads an industrial landscape created by the iron and steel industry which is centred east of the town where the Frodingham ore beds outcropped, masked only by a thin layer of easily removed sand.

Miles of rail sidings serving an industrial panorama of blast furnaces and rolling mills plus ancillary plant provide fascination, if not scenic interest, until our route breasts a second escarpment at Santon and immediately returns to rural peace as we descend at 1 in 95 down a curving alignment through wooded sand warren land to pass Appleby. The station here closed in 1967 but the level-crossing sees us cross the Lincoln–York section of the Roman Ermine Street.

Bowling downhill we soon reach level land again and find ourselves in the Ancholme Valley, crossing both the new and old river courses. Rich arable land, now well drained, takes our immediate eye with a distant view to the left of the steep escarpment of the Lincolnshire Wolds.

Some trains call at Elsham (31$\frac{3}{4}$ miles), where the Lincoln–Barton road is crossed and this is a convenient railhead for Elsham Hall and Country Park, the family seat of the Elwes family and whose gardens and wildlife attractions are open daily to the public.

A climb now follows through a spur of the Lincolnshire Wolds to reach Wrawby Junction, where we are joined by the lines from Retford and Newark. Half a mile of sidings brings us to Barnetby (34$\frac{1}{2}$ miles), our next stop. Once a Wolds agricultural village, it became a railway settlement through the convergence of the three routes here to pursue an easy route to Grimsby and Cleethorpes through the shallow defile of the Barnetby Gap.

Our journey resumes with a climb up to a summit at Melton Ross sidings. The chalk pits on the left have ceased to have any rail connection; on our right, before the A18 overbridge, there is a view of the Humberside Airport at Kirmington.

We are now on a well-used section of line, normally busy with bulk commodities to and from Immingham (imported Swedish iron ore bound for Scunthorpe, imported and refined petroleum products from Killingholme, coal imports and exports through Immingham) and steel traffic to and from Grimsby Docks. A descent at 1 in 200 brings us to Brocklesby (39$\frac{1}{4}$ miles), where the disused station buildings on the right, in ornate stone, are a reminder of the station's early connection with the Yarborough family at Brocklesby Park. Brocklesby Station today sees little traffic but is convenient for a group of villages nearby.

The freight lines to Immingham now diverge left and we continue our journey through woodland of the Brocklesby Estate to reach Habrough (41 miles), pass-enger railhead for the growing port of Immingham and the point at which we join the Humberlink Barton–Cleethorpes route.

SHEFFIELD–RETFORD–BARNETBY

by Devon Baillie and Cyril J. Clark

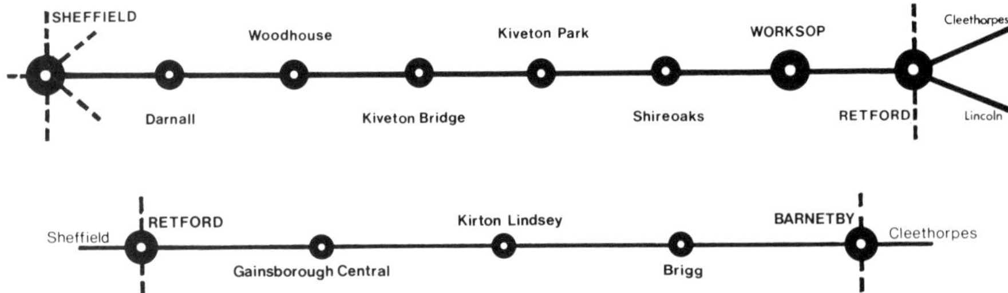

Passenger trains from Sheffield to Retford, Cleethorpes and Lincoln run for the first 10 miles through industrial South Yorkshire, sharing the route with steady freight traffic. After Kiveton Park the line crosses into Nottinghamshire's more rural Bassetlaw District. To the right the Chesterfield Canal, which becomes navigable east of Worksop, comes into view. Just over the hill to the north is the Lindrick gold course, scene of the British Ryder Cup victory over the USA in 1957 – a feat so rare it was not achieved again until a combined British and European team won in 1985.

Shireoaks is a pleasant stone-built village by the River Ryton, on which there is a ford, with a seventeenth-century hall nearby. Just beyond Shireoaks Station is a triangular junction with a line which is now freight-only, for 'Merry-go-Round' coal trains from a number of central Nottinghamshire collieries, but which was used by a passenger service from Nottingham to Worksop via Hucknall, Mansfield and Shirebrook, until it was killed off by Dr Beeching. With goods sidings on either side, a Tesco superstore on the left and a wagon repair shed on the right, we draw into Worksop.

Worksop, serving a town of 37,000 people, is the largest station on the line, and the only one still fully staffed. Worksop Station's architecture resembles that of a Jacobean manor house and is a fitting gateway to the town, which contains some imposing Georgian and Victorian buildings and the fine Priory Church and Gatehouse dating from Norman times. Workshop also has a thriving market, and can be a useful starting point for cycling trips southwards to Welbeck Abbey, Sherwood Forest and Clumber Park – the last of these being 4000 acres of parkland, woodland and a lake, open to the public with good visitor facilities.

After leaving Worksop, our train passes over the A57 Liverpool–Skegness road at Manton Colliery, with its sidings access leading off in a backwards direction on our right. We make our way through flat but very green fields to Retford, passing the site of Ranby Halt, long since closed, immediately prior to running under the Great North Road, and on to Retford, over two sets of level-crossings at Babworth, with its historic links with the Pilgrim Fathers.

If our train is one of those which terminate at Retford, it usually runs into platform 2 of the high-level station, which is reached by continuing on a single track from Whisker Hill Junction, and round a series of tortuous curves to the main station. Through trains use the low-level platform 4, built as part of the dive-under works of 1965, necessary to allow the numerous heavy coal trains to West Burton and Cottam power-stations to pass under the East Coast Main Line.

To the north-east of the station is the centre of East Retford (to give it its proper name), whose focal point is a spacious, pedestrianised market square and the beautiful church of St Swithins. Historic inns remind us of the town's prosperity during coaching days on the Great North Road; and the Chesterfield Canal makes its way through the town in interesting fashion, including an aqueduct and embankment over the valley of the River Idle. Retford's importance for travellers was increased by the opening of the Great Northern Railway in 1849 and the establishment of two depots for a large number of steam locomotives. These have now gone, but Retford remains a calling point for High Speed Trains on the East Coast Main Line.

We almost immediately pass Thrumpton signal-box, with its lifting barriers, and climb a fairly steep gradient to Clarborough Tunnel. On emerging from this we come to Clarborough Junction (now remotely-controlled from Thrumpton), where we see tracks going off to the right. This is the former MS&LR branch to Sykes Junction (opened 1850) and originally carried the Sheffield–Lincoln service. It was closed on 2 November 1959, since when the Sheffield–Lincoln trains have been diverted via Gainsborough Lea Road. However, the line was subsequently reopened as far as Cottam, to serve the coal-fired power station there.

Continuing our journey, we pass the site of Sturton Station ($6\frac{1}{4}$ miles), where only the station house remains, and then approach another large industrial site in the form of West Burton power-station on the right. This has its own signal-box controlling the extensive sidings for coal and ash trains. Soon we see another line coming in on the left – the former GN&GE Joint Line from Doncaster (opened 1867), which bisects the GC line here. The two routes cross the River Trent on common tracks over an iron bridge, and once over the bridge we are in Lincolnshire.

Almost immediately we pass the brick-built Trent Junction signal-box (opened in 1965 to replace a wooden structure on the opposite side of the track), and the GN&GE Joint Line then diverges to the right on its way to Gainsborough's main station (Lea Road), and Lincoln.

Meanwhile, on the left-hand side we pass Dalgety-Spillers' provender mill, and, after passing over four bridges, come to rest in Gainsborough Central Station ($10\frac{1}{4}$ miles), flanked on the left by Marshall's extensive Britannia Works. Once the chief station in Gainsborough, the station building has now been demolished,

Older type of diesel train at Worksop. (*Photo*: Robin Stewart-Smith)

leaving only the signal-box, platforms, footbridge and 'bus-type' shelters. It is an unstaffed halt, with three passenger trains each way per day, but very convenient for the town centre.

Gainsborough is of ancient foundation: in 868 Alfred the Great was married here to Elswitha, daughter of Ethelred, chief of the Ganii; the Danes landed here in 1013 under King Sweyn. In the Middle Ages the town expanded as a result of the wool trade and from the seventeenth century onwards it flourished as an inland port, the long Trent riverfront taking on the highly commercial appearance it has had ever since. A port development association is proposing further upgrading – it is hoped that elimination of the Morton bends in the river will enable more and larger coasters to berth at Gainsborough.

Recent years have seen some erosion of traditional engineering industries, but the transfer of the former Leyland tractor production line from Bathgate, Scotland, to Gainsborough means that the only British-made agricultural tractors are now manufactured in this Lincolnshire town.

The visitor to Gainsborough should not miss the Old Hall (an Elizabethan manor house, now a museum, open 10 a.m.–5 p.m. weekdays and 2 p.m.–5 p.m. Sundays, Easter–October) and All Saints' Parish Church (a Georgian edifice built on to the original fourteenth-century tower). Market days are on Tuesday and Saturday.

Another remarkable feature of this town is that it has the largest model railway layout in the country, in the premises of the Model Railway Society in a former school on Florence Terrace. This is open to the public on special occasions, bank holidays etc. Nine operators are required to run the trains, which are scheduled to strict timetable with regulation signals and bell codes. The models are 'O' gauge and based on the King's Cross–Leeds route.

Finally, the visitor who is well-versed in English literature will know Gainsborough as the 'St Oggs' in George Eliot's *Mill on the Floss*, in which she describes the curious bore which comes up the river in springtime, to a height of several feet. Theatre-goers may also know that Gainsborough was the birthplace, in 1882, of the eminent actress Dame Sybil Thorndike.

On departing from Gainsborough we pass over another bridge and shortly see the Gainsborough High School and Technical College block on the left. Crossing another bridge, over Thonock Lane (rebuilt in 1983), we enter a single-line section. Soon we enter a deep cutting and on emerging see the village of Blyton to the left, with St Martin's Church. A little farther on we pass the site of Blyton station (14¾ miles), which again now comprises only the station house. Continuing through the rural environment, we next come to Northorpe signal-box on the right (17¾ miles), controlling a level-crossing and a passing loop. Here, too, the station is no more.

The next station still open is Kirton Lindsey (20½ miles) – short for Kirton-in-Lindsey, which lies to our right-hand side. This station has been reduced to one platform alongside the single line. A few minutes' walk brings us to the pleasant village of Kirton-in-Lindsey, whose red-brick houses, interspersed with greens, straggle down the steep west side of Lincoln Edge to a squat church typical of this part of the county.

At the top of the ridge, on the southern edge of Kirton, is an RAF station – no longer an operational air base but the home of the Light Air Defence. During the Falklands War the regiment was flown to the islands to provide anti-aircraft cover with its Rapier missiles.

For the cyclist arriving at Kirton, one recommended ride is a 5½-mile trip over the ridge and eastwards along the B1205 to Brandy Wharf on the River Ancholme. There a lovely and unique riverside pub boasts almost every variety of cider available from its cellar. This ride could then be continued to the station at Market Rasen or Brigg.

On leaving Kirton Lindsey Station the train goes into a deepening cutting which culminates in Kirton Tunnel, taking us under Lincoln Edge close to the tower mill. Emerging from the tunnel we see Kirton Cement Works on our right, with Kirton Lime Sidings signal-box on our left, a very lofty wooden structure, no doubt to give the signalman visibility along the line over the top of an adjacent road bridge, under which we pass. We come out of the cutting, and the line resumes double track. We next pass the site of yet another closed station, Scawby and Hibaldstow (24 miles) – the former village was $1\frac{1}{2}$ miles away, the latter $\frac{3}{4}$ mile!

We have now left the high land and travel across the flat, rich land of the Ancholme Valley. The extensive Brigg sugar-beet factory looms up on our left and, after crossing a bridge spanning the River Ancholme, we run into Brigg Station ($26\frac{3}{4}$ miles). The compact market town of Glanford Brigg (to give it its full name) is on the left-hand side of the line. It is a bustling place on market day (Thursday), but there are also quiet walks along tree-lined streets and by the river, which is popular with anglers.

One of Humberside County Council's recommended cycle routes goes north from Brigg, past Wrawby (post mill open to the public), Elsham Country Park and via a string of picturesque villages to South Ferriby and Barton-on-Humber. Should you have come without a bicycle, you can purchase one direct from the bicycle factory in Brigg!

As our train leaves Brigg Station we pass a signal-box on the right which controls a level-crossing and the track becomes single again. We see the Lincolnshire Wolds ahead as we proceed towards Barnetby.

In March 1989 a closure proposal was published for services between Gainsborough and Barnetby. Some politicians and civil servants are determined to push ahead with a new round of rail closures and 'bustitution'. This route is a test case.

DERBY–NOTTINGHAM–LINCOLN
by Malcolm Goodall and Basil Hewis

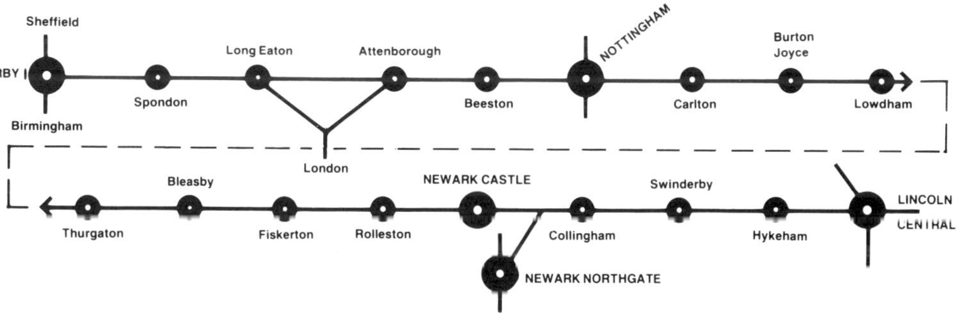

In 1988 British Rail's provincial sector began to develop an hourly Express service between Birmingham and Lincoln, passing through Derby and Nottingham. Frequencies are doubled over this central section. As we leave Derby Station, with the Royal Infirmary and workshops of BREL(1988) Ltd. close by, we cross the junction with the line to Crewe and the tracks from Birmingham on which our Express train entered the station before reversal. Industry dominates the landscape as the route curves past the Railway Technical Centre, where an interesting array of experimental and prototype rolling stock is kept.

Soon we see to the south the rail-connected Courtauld's textile plant and power-station, with Spondon Station conveniently adjoining. Near Borrowash, between the railway and the parallel main road of Roman origin, the enthusiast may spot traces of the long-defunct Derby Canal, before the train passes Church Wilne waterworks, which purifies water extracted from the Derwent for distribution to Nottingham. On the outskirts of Long Eaton the M1 motorway crosses on an overbridge.

Long Eaton is a busy suburban station with a large car park, and has Barton bus connections to the East Midlands airport and aeropark, and the Erewash Valley towns of Sandiacre, Stapleford and Ilkeston. Shardlow canal museum is only 3 miles away by taxi or bicycle. Its ancient warehouses show the volume of goods trans-shipped between river and canal craft when Brindley's route was opened to the Potteries and Merseyside.

Beyond Long Eaton comes the quaintly-named Sheet Stores Junction. The line diverging southwards leads to Castle Donington power-station, where white clouds of water vapour issue from the cooling towers. The brick warehouses on the north side were the central tarpaulin depot for the Midland Railway, but now their canal dock forms a marina for pleasure craft.

Just to the east, we pass the Trent junctions, where a picturesque island platform existed surrounded by green fields until it was demolished in a 1960s resignalling scheme. The complex junctions here reflect the fact that the railways follow the valleys of the Rivers Derwent, Erewash, Soar and Trent to converge here. East of the Trent junctions the route is very busy, with other Express trains, and services from London and Coventry as well as Derby.

This part of the Trent Valley has extensive gravel pits with barges transporting aggregates around the flooded workings. Abandoned areas form a nature reserve with lakeside walks, conveniently reached from Attenborough Station. Giant cooling towers at Ratcliff-on-Soar power-station belch forth vapour in the distance to form a fluffy white backcloth to the watery scene, reducing the wooded slopes of Redhill into insignificance.

Beeston Station lies some distance from the town centre, but stopping trains find good patronage from surrounding housing and the Plessey electronics factory which manufactures telecommunications equipment. The nearby Shipstone's maltings are typical of many built to process Nottinghamshire sandland barley in the first stage of its conversion into the amber fluids which are well appreciated by players on the rugby pitch adjoining.

As we approach Nottingham, gabled and turretted Victorian lace magnates' houses can be discerned in the Park Estate to the west of the castle; while the Central Television studios soon come into view to the south of the line. A new station has been suggested here, to serve housing, industry, the Queen's Medical Centre and the University. Jesse Boot, founder of the pharmaceutical firm, donated Highfields Park for further education: the concrete tower block and older stone university buildings can be seen at a distance to the north. An international selection of containers at the Freightliner depot demonstrates the railway's important role in goods transport. Boots' complex on the south side includes the original 1932 factory by Sir Owen Williams, greatly admired at the time for its novel construction, generous glazing and spacious layout. R. Hood's article on what to see in Nottingham is on pages 47–8.

It was the extension of the Derby–Nottingham line north-eastwards to Lincoln in 1846 which determined the present site of Nottingham Station, opened on 22 May 1848 to avoid the need for complicated reversing out of the original Carrington Street terminus.

The first train to run from Nottingham to Lincoln was a 16-coach special, full of dignitaries and champagne, taking just over one hour to cover the 33 miles non-stop. Today's trains generally take just over an hour if they call at all the 11 intermediate stations, or $\frac{3}{4}$ hour if calling only at Newark, with an hourly frequency between the two cities.

We leave Nottingham under London Road and over the canal, still used by pleasure craft but which formerly carried goods to and from wharves in the heart of the city. London trains also used to leave in this direction, via Old Dalby and Melton Mowbray! That line closed in 1967, and its iron-girder bridge over the Trent now carries road traffic.

On the left, past the canal, is the old Great Northern Railway's London Road (Low Level) Station, which later became a parcels depot, and was then redeveloped for non-railway use. Thankfully, it is a protected listed building which has been majestically restored.

The once extensive sidings on both sides of the line are rapidly becoming redundant. Much railway archaeology remains for about a mile, in the shape of extensive earthworks, derelict viaducts and bridges, which were part of the Great Northern's outlets from Nottingham Victoria and the two London Road stations (High Level and Low Level) and their connections with the Midland's empire.

On the right, the floodlights of Notts County Football Club and, just behind but across the Trent, Nottingham Forest mark the two closest-sited league football grounds in the country.

As we move out of the inner city area and over Colwick road level-crossing, on the left is a most interesting natural phenomenon: a rare 220-million-year-old cliff-face rock formation which has excited scientists and conservationists. Nottingham City Council has agreed to a request by the Nature Conservancy Council that the 40-foot-high red-coloured face – made up of layers of rock and mud – is preserved. The cliff was formed in the Triassic period, when the River Trent was more than four times its present width, and Nottingham was an area of semi-desert.

On the right is Nottingham Racecourse, which also has an extensive country park.

Just before the first station, Carlton – a busy suburb and shopping area – the Grantham and Skegness line branches off to the right into Netherfield Station. Until Nottingham Victoria closed in 1967, the Great Northern Grantham line ran separately but parallel to our line for two miles before taking to the earthworks previously mentioned. Then the above stations were called Carlton & Netherfield and Netherfield & Colwick – confused?!

The very edge of the built up area is marked by the bridge carrying the former Great Northern outer suburban line which now serves only Gedling Colliery.

The line to Newark is now straight and flat, passing through several almost equally spaced attractive villages – Burton Joyce, Lowdham, Thurgarton, Bleasby, Fiskerton. At Burton Joyce Station we get our first – but certainly not last – view of the Trent, in a majestic 180-degree sweep. The low hills of the edge of the Trent Valley are visible to the right and left across the flat flood plain. The agriculture and the landscapes, however, are interesting and varied, with plenty of wildlife to be seen: mixed livestock and arable farms with small traditional fields and hedges; woods and extensive lineside ditches with marshes and bulrushes; old and operating gravel workings with extensive lakes; sewage-farm lagoons. These

Historic Newark Castle

stretches of water help to make the Trent Valley an important feeding and stopping place for migrating geese, ducks and waders between the Arctic and European mainland.

The original station buildings at Lowdham and Thurgarton, in an ornate Tudor cottage style, together with the semaphore signalling, give an old world charm to this stretch of the line. Lowdham has a fine public house, The Railway, almost on the platform.

The name 'Fiskerton Junction' on the signal-box between Bleasby and Fiskerton Stations may present a puzzle today, but this marks the spot where the line northwards to Southwell and Mansfield branched off. It formed one third of a huge triangular junction, of which our line formed the second side, and the third was from Southwell south-eastwards to Rolleston Junction – now just Rolleston.

Passenger trains first reached Southwell from Rolleston Junction (a distance of $2\frac{1}{2}$ miles) in 1847, but a regular service was not introduced until 1860, and on to Mansfield in 1871. Southwell Station was then re-built and the original wooden building was transported to form part of Beeston Station! The construction of the line to Mansfield helped to open up the coalfield in that area, and it was to cater for the coal traffic to Nottingham that the spur to Fiskerton Junction was opened in the 1920s.

The Southwell platforms at Rolleston are still there, untouched since the passenger service ceased on 15 June 1959. The area is now a riot of vegetation,

38

young trees and colour in spring and summer, with wild and old garden flowers in profusion – quite a nature reserve.

Rolleston is still the station for the adjacent Southwell Racecourse. The nearest station to the cathedral city of Southwell (with a population of just over 5,000 it is Britain's smallest) is actually Fiskerton.

On the right, Staythorpe power-station, now partially closed, once received 20 coal trains a day, but switched to oil and then to road transport of coal during and after the 1984/5 miners' strike. Needless to say, there is a strong desire locally to revert to rail haulage.

Just beyond the power-station we have a spectacular crossing of the Trent near Staythorpe weir, where the river splits into two sections. The section over which we travel, the Trent proper, undredged, with several islands, sand and gravel banks, and of great wildlife value, skirts round Newark to the north; the two sections join up again a mile or so north of the town. The section which passes through Newark itself is partially canalised and dredged for river traffic – these days mainly pleasure craft. Up to the late 1970s, half a dozen barges a day, mainly carrying oil, were commonplace, and in recent years some bulk freight has returned to the water. Oil is carried on our line, and you may well pass a rake of long tanker wagons. From Newark, trips lasting up to 2 hours can be taken in pleasure launches, with catering facilities, between about Easter and late September.

To the left of the line runs a long stretch of broad swampy ditch which is a marvellous wildlife haven untouched for decades. Newark is entered past the livestock market on the right. Wednesday is market day, with cattle, pigs and sheep in great numbers. So important has Newark become for cattle that moves are afoot to seek a larger site. The castle is clearly visible behind the cattle market, dominating the river.

Castle Station is closer to the historic centre of Newark than the town's other station, Northgate, on the East Coast Main Line. A short walk brings you across the river to the castle remains, dating from 1170, in attractive grounds which are open all year. The castle itself is currently being restored, although a small exhibition in the south-west tower is open on Wednesdays and Fridays.

Also worth a visit is the Millgate Museum of Folk Life and its craft workshops. History and the present day come together in the large cobbled market square, with its stalls on Wednesday, Friday and Saturday against a background of many notable buildings, including the Governor's House, Moot Hall and beautiful fourteenth-century Old White Hart. There are bus services from Newark to Southwell and to Winthorpe with its extensive collection of historic aircraft.

As the train leaves Newark you can see evidence of considerable past freight activity; but the sidings are now lifted, and the coalyard and British Sugar Corporation factory now served by road. We now cross the new A46 bypass.

Over the Trent again we go in spectacular fashion, over the weirs and locks on the canalised section, and on towards a very rare piece of railway engineering – the famous or infamous flat crossing, which the East Coast Main Line approaches from the north on a latticed iron-girder bridge. In the very early days, the Great Northern Railway was prepared to let the Midland control the crossing, giving the Midland priority, believing from the outset that the other company's traffic would be insignificant. However, friction persisted, and still does, over 60 years after the companies' demise. Drivers of today's Nottingham–Lincoln trains can still be heard to curse the Great Northern if they are held up by something on the East Coast Main Line, especially if it is a slow ballast train.

Beyond the flat crossing, we are joined by a spur from the main line, laid in 1965, which takes the Newark Northgate–Cleethorpes services and the daily

High Speed Train between Cleethorpes and King's Cross. Shortly we go under the Great North Road and take a final look at the Trent as it heads north while we go north-east.

Collingham Station, in an area of five level-crossings within a mile or so, has an impressive building (now a private house) of 'Italianate-cum-Greek' style, in marked contrast to the Tudor style at Lowdham and Thurgarton. The desolate arm of a loading gauge and the earthworks of a loading ramp and bay remind us that goods traffic was once part of the life of this station. The delightful village of Collingham is the last we see in Nottinghamshire, as the line passes into Lincolnshire, through gently undulating arable farmland, with stretches of woodland from time to time. Two more unstaffed stations, Swinderby and Hykeham are served, and we are then in the built-up area of Lincoln, with the first impressive view of that city's three-towered cathedral, dominating it to the north.

About two miles from Lincoln the train slows to negotiate a severe curve to the left, away from the original Midland line. This is the Boultham curve, laid in 1984 and opened in May 1985 to enable the former Midland station of Lincoln St Marks to be closed and all trains to use the larger and better-appointed Central Station. The curve takes us on to the Doncaster line and we approach Lincoln from the west, over Brayford Pool, bustling with pleasure craft, and into the handsome stone-built Central Station.

A WALK AROUND LINCOLN
by Ron Everett

The city of Lincoln (population 75,000) is best known for its 900-year-old cathedral, but it contains many other interesting historic monuments which can be seen on a walk from Central Station.

Cross the road outside the station and bear left into the pedestrian precinct. Along your route of about four miles (which can of course be shortened, using the city-centre plan) stand many markers of the city's chequered history: an inland harbour developed by the Romans; Saxon churches; a Norman castle and cathedral; two very different museums – one housed in the former Lincs Yeomanry barracks, the second in the thirteenth-century church of a Franciscan friary; a working windmill; an art gallery. Each centre welcomes visitors.

Adjacent to the station is the beautiful St Mary-le-Wigford Church. Don't just admire the Anglo-Saxon tower – call in. This is a church information centre. Just along Wigford Way is Brayford Marina. It is almost impossible now to imagine the wharves bustling with the woollen trade of the Middle Ages or the later grain traffic. The warehouses and barge traffic disappeared in the 1960s. From the North Wharf, embark for a pleasure boat ride or visit the National Cycle Museum. Glance up the hill to the older part of the city: it is easy to understand why our ancestors preferred living on the easily fortified hilltop.

The riverside walk through the Glory Hole takes you back to High Street, almost opposite the Tourist Information Centre. Through the Stonebow, site of the old city south gate, climb Steep Hill past craft, book and antique shops to Castle Square. Thankfully, refreshment is easy to find. An enquiring visitor will find anything less than half a day inadequate to explore the castle and cathedral.

An original of Magna Carta and the infamous Imp are just two cathedral treasures.

Take a short walk along Westgate to the old barracks on Burton Road to see Lincolnshire's agricultural, military and industrial past. Steam diggers, ploughs, threshing machines – sometimes in steam, farming tableaux and artefacts share galleries alongside the museum collection of the Royal Lincolnshire Regiment. Just around the corner, in Mill Road, the Ellis windmill grinds flour for its visitors at weekends.

Begin to retrace your steps along Westgate. Making your way to the Bail via Chapel Lane you pass under the only Roman arch, Newport Arch – still spanning a public highway. Throughout this area watch out for excavated archaeological sites. Through Cathedral Close to Greestone Stairs brings you to the delightful Usher Galley with its collection of watches, porcelain and art objects.

On the right, as you continue down Lindum Hill, is the City and County Museum, housed in a thirteenth-century friary, the home of archaeology, armoury and natural history exhibits. Conclude your circular tour by walking back to High Street, along Waterside North through the newly laid-out City Square. Breathless? City Transport normally do regular city bus tours during the summer for the less energetic!

Shoppers in Lincoln High Street. (*Photo*: Peter Cronin)

NEWARK–LINCOLN–CLEETHORPES
by Ron Everett

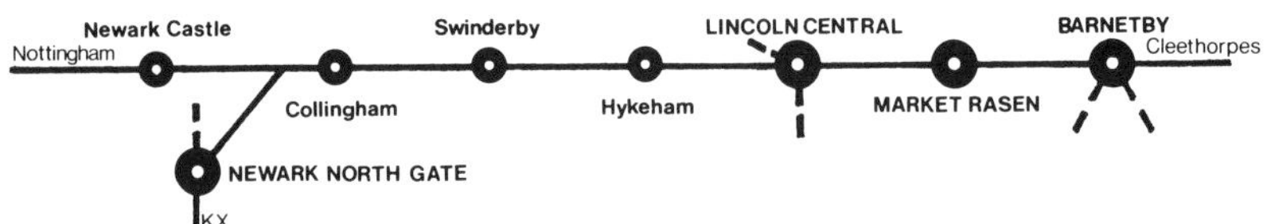

No traveller would normally be in a hurry to leave the historic town of Newark-upon-Trent, with its riverside walks, boats for hire and medieval churches, especially on a Wednesday when the bustling market is in full swing. Should you be travelling on to Lincoln or South Humberside, there is a good service from the former Great Northern Northgate Station. Based on roughly two-hourly intervals, the service is designed to connect with East Coast Main Line services. Once a day, the 'Humber–Lincs' High Speed Train provides a through service, leaving Cleethorpes in the morning for London, returning in the evening.

Northgate Station, although farther from the town centre than the former Midland Railway's Castle Station, is the one from which we depart. Thanks to the financial co-operation of the local authorities with British Rail, facilities have been upgraded. Seating and waiting accommodation has been renewed on the 'up' platform, and vending machines installed. The much enlarged car-parking area bears testimony to the popularity of the High Speed Train service. Because so many people may drive from Lincoln to Newark to catch the train, in the early 1990s air-conditioned Class 158 units will take over this service, and line speeds have been raised. Just before the flat Newark crossing of two rail routes, with the girder work of the Trent bridge looming up, our train takes the 1965-laid spur to join the ex-Midland line to Lincoln. Details of the journey from here to Lincoln will be found on page 40.

As a provincial centre for the day-tripper, weekend visitor or longer-stay tourist, Lincoln has much to offer. A more detailed description is given in the section on pages 40–41. For the serious walker, Lincoln, with its ideally sited youth hostel, is a convenient intermediate point for the long-distance footpath from Oakham to the Humber – the Viking Way. Guides of the path are stocked at libraries or information centres in the county.

The geographical nature of the area determined that all railways travelled east–west through Lincoln, to avoid the heights. Incredibly, seven lines converged to take the Witham Gap in the city. Central Station was the meeting place for most of these lines and it was, with the generous help of the City council, refurbished in 1985. A new booking hall opened in 1988.

Our train now takes the left-hand curve laid by the Great Central Railway constituent company, the Manchester, Sheffield & Lincolnshire Railway Company, in 1848. We also pass under the Pelham Road bridge – built in 1958 to replace a level-crossing and help relieve the city's severe traffic congestion.

Veering away to the right of the diesel depot, built on the site of the former GCR steam shed, is the GN&GE Joint Line to Sleaford (with connections on to the Nottingham–Skegness branch), Spalding and Peterborough. The diverted 'Night Scotsman' came to grief here on the night of 3 June 1962. Exceeding a speed restriction by 40 mph, the down express jumped the rails and three people were killed in the accident.

Our train rattles across the River Witham, meandering its way to Boston, and the view transforms from heavy-engineering works to open agricultural country

Sprinter between Lincoln and Market Rasen at Snelland. (*Photo:* Peter Cronin)

once more. With the exception of Market Rasen, all intermediate stations between Lincoln and Barnetby have been closed. Usselby closed in 1960, the remaining eight, five years later. The recent fortunes of the line have been chequered.

Following the laying of the 1965 connecting spur at Newark, iron-ore trains travelled this way to Scunthorpe steel works. In 1973, the transportation of this low-grade ore ceased. However, by this time, displaced trains from the closed East Lincolnshire line were using the route. Passenger trains share the rails with block oil-trains from the South Humberside refineries.

In the rather featureless scenery of this part of West Lindsey, you could be excused for beginning to doze. Behind the tranquil calm, however, a quite revolution has taken place. 'Black gold' has been discovered in commercial quantities. Oil from the wells is pumped into storage tanks at Langworth, 7 miles from Lincoln, from where it is transported for refining. Three train-loads per week are anticipated as production rises.

As the train brakes for the stop at sleepy Market Rasen (population 2,500), note once again how the landscape has begun to change. The wolds and wooded areas to the east are far more attractive than large fields with their hedges grubbed out. Keep a look-out for low-flying aircraft.

Rasen is a useful railhead for walkers. Apart from the Viking Way, the Forestry Commission plantations offer families, or those with limited time to spare, pleasant forest walks, with picnic areas, up to eight miles in length. On the A631, to the east of the town, the National Hunt racecourse is set against a backcloth of Willingham Woods. For cyclists there are plenty of quiet roads with only the gentlest of gradients to the south and west; or more challenging (but not exhausting) rides eastwards over the wolds via the historic towns of Caistor or Louth to the railheads of Habrough, Grimsby or Cleethorpes.

Geographical contours soon dictate the rail route again. To gain access to the coastal plain east of the wolds, the line proceeds north and north-west before swinging east at Wrawby Junction – where the lines from Scunthorpe and Sheffield converge – to the station of Barnetby-le-Wold in the Melton Gap. The sheer size of this village station, with its two island platforms, emphasises how much the Great Central over-estimated the potential of Barnetby as a railway junction. This is the railhead for Kirmington (Humberside) airport.

Beyond Barnetby, industrial buildings once again begin to dominate the skyline, and the railway itself becomes noticeably busier. Of the growing commuter villages, our train will only stop at Habrough before pulling into Grimsby Town about 80 minutes from Newark. The seaside terminus of Cleethorpes, only a further $3\frac{1}{4}$ miles, will take another ten short, but interesting, minutes. (See sections on Doncaster–Cleethorpes and Humberlink.)

PETERBOROUGH–NOTTINGHAM
by Colin Hawthorn and D. Taylor-Smith

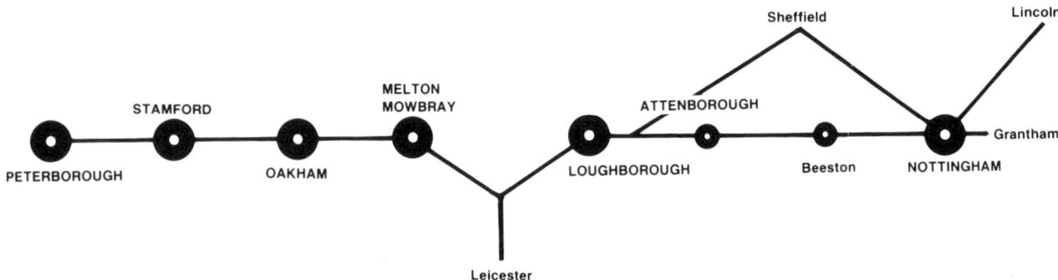

In May 1988 British Rail's Provincial managers introduced their new Express services linking East Anglia and the north-west at hourly intervals through Nottingham and Sheffield. Comfortable Class 156 Sprinters provide the service, travelling from Peterborough to Nottingham through Grantham, thence north to Sheffield, though some trains diverge to serve Derby. The route from Peterborough to Grantham is covered in Chapter 3, and that from Grantham to Nottingham in Chapter 4.

From 1990 the intention is to use faster air-conditioned Class 158 units routed through Melton Mowbray. This chapter describes that journey, due to start in 1990.

Leaving the modern Peterborough Station, which attracts hundreds of shoppers daily to the adjacent Queensgate Centre, our train runs on tracks alongside the East Coast Main Line for six miles. Our tracks through flat fen country were built first, by the Midland Railway, followed by the main line tracks of the Great Northern Railway, which was not allowed to build stations at Walton or Helpston.

As we turn westward, we soon see to our left the spacious grounds of Burghley House, now known by televising of the annual Burghley Horse Trials. Lord Burghley kept the Great Northern main line from coming to Stamford, which kept the town relatively small, in comparison with the growth of Peterborough. By 1855 he had relented and built his own line, from Essendine to a fine stone-built terminus in Water Street, which we pass. The Great Northern once also had a branch from Stamford to Wansford.

A stone-faced cutting and short tunnel under St Martin's High Street bring us into Stamford Midland Station, an ideal starting point for a walk around the town. Walking away from the station, turning left and avoiding Station Road, we soon reach Stamford Meadows, from where we have a good view of the town, rising above river level, with its church spires against the skyline. A short walk, crossing the George footbridge over the River Welland, and then a second one over the mill-stream, with the Town Road bridge on our right, brings us up a narrow road to the Market Place, shops and cafés and the old Great North Road, the traffic now thankfully using the by-pass. When Stamford was on the main road from London to Edinburgh, many travellers sang its praises, the novelist Sir Walter Scott describing St Mary's Hill as 'the finest scene between London and Edinburgh'. St Mary's is one of six noteworthy churches in the town centre, which also contains many excellent town houses of local stone which have been featured on television.

The High Street is now a pedestrian precinct, and the residential roads climb to the higher ground, with some side-turnings of surprising steepness: it is possible to be quite suddenly on a level half-way up with a church tower. The height above sea level varies from 80 to 200 feet. Browne's Hospital (1475) is a building of interest, in Broad Street, as is the Grammar School and Chapel (1532); also St Leonard's Priory (1082) and the Whitefriars Gate (1475), now one of the entrances to the hospital.

Leaving Stamford, we pass under the concrete A1 road overbridge and out of Lincolnshire into Leicestershire. To our left lies the River Welland and soon to our right we see the Ketton cement works, with its rail connection. Thence past Ketton village, its church, like so many in this area, graced by a large spire. At the closed station of Luffenham, we see to our left the club-house of Luffenham Heath Golf Club and we cross over the Leicester–Stamford road.

Soon we reach the junction at Manton, where the freight route from Corby trails in on our left. During 1988 the junction was rebuilt to remove the notorious 10 mph speed restriction which checked all westbound trains just as they plunged into Manton Tunnel. Climbing out of the tunnel, it is but two miles to Oakham, past an arm of Rutland Water, a man-made reservoir complex notable for its sporting activities.

The market town of Oakham (6,400) was the capital of England's smallest county, Rutland, which was swallowed up by Leicestershire in the 1974 reorganisation of local government. Oakham Station is now the only passenger station left in the former county of Rutland, and is the railhead for a wide rural area. The town is at the southern end of the 120-mile Viking Way – a long-distance footpath through Lincolnshire to the Humber Bridge. A short walk along this path brings you to Burley Wood and the banks of Rutland Water.

Oakham is a graceful, peaceful town with much to offer: museum, farm park with rare breeds, school, and a castle – really the Great Hall of the castle, perfectly preserved and used as the local court. Its walls are covered by horseshoes, but no normal ones – many of these are huge. By custom, every peer (and that includes Queen Victoria and Queen Elizabeth II) who enters the county must hand over a horseshoe. Oakham also has an ancient Grammar School, founded in 1584 by Archdeacon Johnson (who also founded the nearby public school at Uppingham) and which has tripled in size in recent years. A well-known hostelry in Oakham is the Crown Hotel, an old building extensively modernised and with its accommodation increased.

From Oakham the line heads north through Ashwell – where once there were sidings built to exploit the local iron ore, and Whissendine, and then swings west at the closed station of Saxby, formerly junction of the Midland & Great Northern Joint Railway which ran across Lincolnshire and Norfolk to Yarmouth until its closure in 1959. This carried a daily Leicester–Yarmouth train and a service from Spalding to Nottingham.

We also pass Stapleford Park, where Lord Harborough objected to the Midland Railway building over his land. For this reason the original line was sharply curved, and had to be realigned in 1892 when it became an express route from St Pancras.

Approaching Melton Mowbray, the Pedigree Petfoods factory is on the right, with a siding opened in February 1986, with the aid of a government grant, to enable its products to be sent out by rail in familiar brown curtain-sided containers. Another link to the factory for raw materials was later built from the goods-yard west of the station.

Melton is a very gracious town of 17,000 people; it is clustered round the magnificent St Mary's Church, which is well worth a visit. The town has one of the largest cattle markets in the UK where almost anything, from a Stilton cheese to a cow, a ton of hay to a canary, can be bought. The retail market continues to spread along the town centre and new shops are constantly being built. Pork pies are a famous local product, but the town is also notable as headquarters for the Royal Army Veterinary Corps, Pedigree Petfoods and a major shipping line (the sea is actually some 90 miles away).

West of the station, you can see the Old Dalby test track, once a through route to Nottingham direct, before the train runs down the fertile Wreake Valley.

Man first made his mark in Leicestershire 4,000 years ago as he walked up the Wreake. Along its valley lie villages like Hoby, Thrussington, Rotherby and Frisby, all with lovely ironstone churches and houses and old brick cottages. John Ferneley, the great nineteenth-century horse painter, was born at Thrussington. To the south are the uplands with Burrough Hill, an ancient hill fort and racecourse, Pickwell and Gadesby. Between Hoby and Rotherby are the remains of the Wreake Canal, built in 1794.

At Syston, the train sharply reduces speed as it negotiates the tight curve leading to the Midland Main Line. Syston is the northern limit of the suburbs of Leicester, but our train does not enter the city. Instead we accelerate northwards towards Nottingham, passing Sileby and below Barrow-upon-Soar – each of which once had a station. Sileby is a large shoe-making village; now large estates wrap around two sides like a crescent. The church is lovely, as is that of Barrow, which nestles alongside the Soar. To the east are upland wolds with attractive villages like Ratcliffe and Seagrave, while to the west is Rothley, with its Saxon cross, ancient Bradgate Park, where the ill-fated Lady Jane Grey lived, and lovely Swithland reservoir – best seen from the Great Central Railway. It is hard to realise that it is man-made, with the swans, ducks and reed beds.

The Trip to Jerusalem inn nestles under Nottingham's Castle Rock

Between Sileby and Barrow-upon-Soar, on the left, is a Redland Stone depot, where Mountsorrel granite is loaded into hopper wagons and transported by train to many parts of the country.

Farther on, also on the left, can be seen the Leicester Navigation – a canal originally built to carry coal – and soon after, on the right, is Loughborough Chord Junction, linking to the main line a remnant of the old Great Central route retained to serve the British Gypsum Works at Hotchley Hill.

Loughborough, population 45,000, is now more of a city than an industrial town. Famous for its Carillion and bell foundry, it also contains the Brush (Hawker-Siddley) factory, on the right of the line, where many British Rail locomotives and components have been made. Loughborough's former College of Advanced Technology is now an expanding university, noted for technological and physical education; and there is an equally famous College of Design. Loughborough Station was recently improved with the help of a County Council grant – the brickwork has been cleaned, the up-side waiting room enlarged and 180 trees and shrubs planted on the station approach.

Beyond Loughborough, the train passes Hathern and Kegworth. We soon see Radcliffe-on-Soar power-station to the right, before plunging into the short Redhill Tunnels, and approaching Trent Junction. The last few miles into Nottingham are described on page 36.

NOTTINGHAM

by R. Hood

General Booth, Torville and Dean, Raleigh, Players and Boots. Household names, all of them from the city that prides itself on being the 'Queen of the Midlands'. Forget about other places. Buy your ticket, hop on the train and speed your way to Nottingham. This is the place to be, and has been ever since prehistoric man first made a snug home for himself on the sandstone cliffs above Narrow Marsh. That's how it came to be known as Tigcuocobaucc, which means houses of caves.

Later settlers sailed their craft up the Trent, couldn't pronounce this tongue-twister and changed it to the homestead of their leader, an Anglo-Saxon gentleman who rejoiced in the name of Snot (somehow the 'S' got lost for the city, but survives in the suburb of Sneinton).

There's always plenty to see and do. Ride round the centre on the 600 or 700 buses to get the feel of the place, then spend all day window shopping. Don't forget to search out some Colwick cheese, spread it thickly on bread and butter, douse liberally with vinegar and devour greedily. Grab a fistful of leaflets from the information office in Wheeler Gate (closed Sunday) and dive underground for a guided tour of the city caves, to see where it all started. Escape from this claustrophobia to one of the central parks. Take your seat at Trent Bridge and listen to the sound of willow on leather; or catch the bus to the broad expanse of Wollaton Park, stroll by the lake and admire the herds of deer. If it rains, dash inside the palatial hall and marvel at the natural history exhibits. The insect section is particularly good, but if creepy-crawlies give you the heeby-jeebies then head across the stable yard to the Industrial Museum, with its steam engines, lace machinery and other contrivances that helped the city to prosperity.

Having acquired a taste for the past, head back to the town and drop in at the Brewhouse Yard to see household scenes of yesteryear, and a collection of weird and wonderful potions in the old chemist's shop. Don't forget to look round the spooky cellars. Climb up to the Castle grounds for the view; inside is the Fine Arts Museum. Just down Castle Road is one of the few remaining timber-framed buildings, saved in the nick of time and restored to house a dazzling display of Nottingham lace. See how it was made in the Lace Hall, and applied for adornment in the Costume Museum; then brave the traffic on Maid Marian Way to get to Canal Street and the Pickfords warehouse, its watery recesses telling the story of inland navigation. Exhausted by all this, recover in the Fellows Morton and Clayton, which brews its own beer.

Wondering what to do in the evening? There are night clubs and discos, while the cosmopolitan population presents a varied international cuisine. Glide on to the ice rink, knock hell out of the tenpins in the bowling alley opposite, sail at the Holme Pierreport Water Sports Centre, have a dip in the swimming baths – or, for a more leisurely pastime, wander through the lace market and marvel at the brickwork canyons created by eminent architects to house the lace trade. Queue for seats at the magnificent concert hall or hasten to the October Goose Fair. Then ... but I've run out of space. Jump on the train to Nottingham and see for yourself. I'll meet you by the lions in Slab Square!

NOTTINGHAM–SHEFFIELD

by Malcolm Goodall

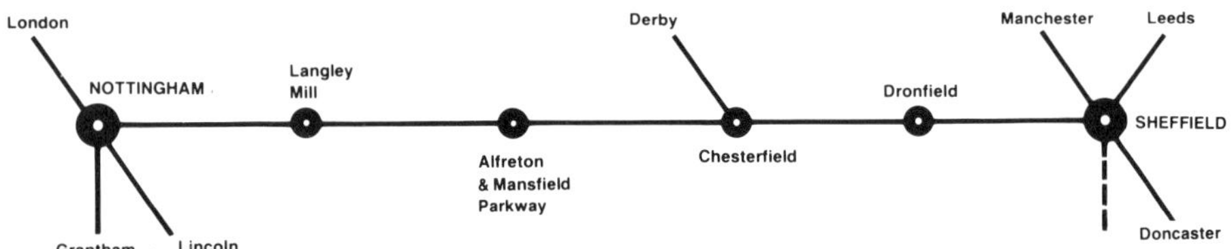

Railway services around Nottingham reached their nadir after a savage attack by the Beeching axe in the 1960s. One main line was totally shut down, and several branches were lopped, leaving a much reduced network centred on the Midland station at Carrington Street. The outlook was bleak as Nottingham became a dead-end for InterCity services, and local authorities eagerly seized on railway routes as cheap building land instead of retaining them as valuable transport assets for the future.

Recently, however, there has been something of a rail renaissance in the city, largely due to initiatives by the energetic Provincial sector management. Reopening of the Mansfield line is under study, and there are even plans for a new light railway transit system to relieve city road congestion.

Nottingham is now the hub of a network of provincial services operated by modern Sprinter diesel units, fanning out in all directions; the successful Provincial formula of short but frequent trains means that there are now more daily departures than in the 1960s, when more lines were open. The Lincoln–Derby–Birmingham service runs hourly, increased to half-hourly on the Nottingham–Derby section. Stopping trains run every two hours or so to Grantham and Skegness. May 1988 saw the introduction of a new hourly stopping service to Leicester and Coventry (complementing InterCity's London trains as far as Leicester), and also the hourly Express route from East Anglia to Nottingham, Sheffield and the north-west.

Nottingham's fine Edwardian station has been thoroughly modernised to give a good start to our journey. The train crawls out over the reverse curves that mark the site of the original 1839 terminal, and rapidly accelerates past Castle Park, a 'pop-art' piece of architecture for mundane warehousing purposes. Viewed from the air, its coloured gravel paths appear as a pinnacled tower! Prominently on the clifftop stands Nottingham Castle – a ducal mansion built in the 1670s on the site of the old castle which was demolished after the Civil War. It was burnt out in the Reform Bill riots of 1831 and subsequently restored by noted local architect T. C. Hine in 1878 as a museum.

Until May 1990, trains pass south-west through Beeston on the line to Derby and London before curving sharply through the lace-making town of Long Eaton, and slowly through Railfreight Coal's Toton marshalling yards, into the valley of the River Erewash.

At Trowell Junction the direct line from Nottingham trails in from the east. From May 1990, all trains should revert to this shorter route, which passes the marina created on flat ground within sight of Nottingham Castle. The line follows the valley of the River Leen for a mile or so, threading between obsolete factories awaiting redevelopment, and swings sharply westward at Radford where the Raleigh bicycle works are situated. The tracks diverging to the right at Radford lead only to Calverton colliery, but there are plans to use them for both a Sprinter service to Mansfield and a light rail transit route to Hucknall. Where suburbia changes to open countryside beyond Wollaton, coal deposits were reputedly worked in Roman times. Profits from later pits helped finance the building of the impressive Wollaton Hall, completed in 1588 for Sir Francis Willoughby. By 1604, Huntingdon Beaumont had a wooden wagonway operating to carry coal from deeper mines nearby at Strelley – the first ever recorded railway in this country! It seems unfair that this enterprising pioneer's business failed to flourish: Beaumont ended up in Nottingham jail a few years later!

The small River Erewash forms the county boundary and is crossed several times by the railway, which means that potential sites for an Ilkeston station are in Nottinghamshire, although this important town of 33,000 people stands on a Derbyshire hilltop, to the west of the track. A competing route once strode across the valley on the spindly-legged ironwork Bennerley Viaduct, now preserved as an industrial monument but strangely bereft of its approach embankments. Shipley Gate Station has long since disappeared, but the older Boat inn still serves refreshment to canal travellers in a rather isolated location.

Some trains now slow to call at Langley Mill Station, rebuilt and reopened in May 1986 with local authority finance. Walk from here down to the marina at

Blackpool North to Ipswich train stops at Langley Mill. (*Photo:* Malcolm Goodall)

Langley Bridge, formerly an important canal junction and now the head of navigation on the Erewash Canal. Continue up the hill for half a mile to Eastwood, noting the Sun inn at the crossroads, popularly regarded as the birthplace of the Midland Railway. The writer D. H. Lawrence was born in Eastwood and his former home at 8a Victoria Street is now a museum. Many of his novels are set in the surrounding countryside and mining townships. Walk the mile back downhill to the station or catch the frequent Trent bus which is the successor to the tramway which Lawrence used as the setting for his short story *Tickets Please*, later made into a television film.

The train journey northwards from Langley Mill passes the restored gridiron terraces of industrial workers' cottages at Codnor Park and Ironville. Trains of preserved rolling stock may be seen reversing here on the Midland Railway Trust's line, but there is no passenger interchange yet. Some freight traffic does, however, use a connection to reach the Butterley Company's engineering works. This concern used to have coalmines, ironworks, housing and its own private road and rail network: a fascinating hunting ground for the industrial archaeologist. Their best-known product must be the framework of St Pancras Station trainshed, several girders bearing the company's name and date of manufacture.

Very soon, at Pye Bridge Junction, a heavily-used freight line climbs steeply away north-eastwards, curving sharply as it follows the alignment of a former horse-drawn tramway. Rail-freight locomotives haul successive strings of empty coal hoppers up here all day, for refilling at the collieries in Sherwood Forest. This line leads to Ashfield and Mansfield which, with a population approaching a quarter of a million, form the largest conurbation in the country without a train service. Restoration of a service from Nottingham is under study, but for the present Mansfield passengers must continue along the Sheffield line, through the tunnel to Alfreton & Mansfield Parkway Station (built in 1973 on the site of an earlier, closed station with local authority help), and catch a bus for the 8 miles to Mansfield.

Parkway Station is also the railhead for the Midland Railway Trust's line and museum at Butterley; daily buses 242/243 run two or three times every hour. From here, our train has but a short climb to a summit in the mile-long cutting at Morton,and a quick descent to Clay Cross ironworks and junction, where the line from Derby merges in from the south-west, overlooked by the blackened tower of North Wingfield church.

The importance of the coal industry is dramatically illustrated at night by the fiery glow from the coke ovens incongruously named 'Avenue' after the tree-lined coach road from Wingerworth. Smokeless fuel moves by rail from here to the furnaces of Sheffield and to domestic consumers further afield. A mile further on are long brick terraces of railway cottages in 'Midland Gothic' style, now sadly disfigured by their new owners.

Houses and factories herald the approach to the coal and iron town of Chesterfield. As a line from a tube works trails in from the west, the famous crooked spire of All Saints Church can be clearly seen. Legend has it that the devil flew down in a rage at the completion of another symbol of Christianity and twisted his tail round the offending spire, the deformity produced lasting to the present day. A more prosaic explanation is the warping of unseasoned timber. By the small modern station is Markham's engineering works, which built many stationary steam engines used at local mines for winding coal.

Chesterfield, generally thought of as an industrial town, contains much of interest and is well worth a visit. On leaving the station entrance, just head straight for the crooked spire. Walk up Corporation Street past the restored Chesterfield Hotel, over the footbridge across the bypass road, calling in perhaps

The Sun Inn, Eastwood (1 mile from Langley Mill Station). (*Photo:* Malcolm Goodall)

at the Pomegranate Theatre booking office, then into the church grounds. The church dates from 1234 and the nearby market is even older. A pedestrianised shopping centre leads from the church through thoughtfully restored streets to the narrow alleyways of the Shambles and the huge stone-surfaced Market Place, alive with the bustle of trading on Mondays, Fridays and Saturdays, while a collector's flea-market is held on Thursdays.

Walk through the busy Market Hall and contrast this with the modern 'Pavements' complex opposite, a refreshing change from the usual concrete boxes. The Peacock is a sixteenth century timber-framed building on the Pavement frontage to the New Square end of the Market Place, beautifully converted to an information office open Monday to Saturday (Telephone 207777). A heritage centre on the upper floor is now open in the afternoon. A short distance further on, a footbridge leads from New Beetwell Street over the River Hipper to Queen's Park, whose attractions include county cricket, boating, bowls, swimming and tennis.

Chesterfield is a useful base for exploring the Peak District, using buses from the East Midland bus station in New Beetwell Street (Telephone (0246) 211007 or 250450). All Sheffield–London and many north-east to south-west InterCity trains call at Chesterfield in addition to the hourly Express service from East Anglia, and the north-west.

To the north of Chesterfield is the hilltop Tapton House, leased by George Stephenson, the engineer of this line, who amused himself here in his retirement growing hothouse fruits. His North Midland Railway from Derby followed the valley of the little River Rother northwards to maintain its superb alignment, but our route diverges north-westwards towards Sheffield. A stagnant green ditch at Tapton Junction is the uppermost reach of the Chesterfield Canal, engineered by the pioneer Brindley to give an outlet for Peak District lead. After Sheepbridge ironworks comes a rural interlude with rugged stone-built farmsteads clinging to the hillsides.

Dronfield is a rapidly expanding commuter township with the old village as its centre. Its closed station was reopened as an emergency measure in the bad winter weather of 1979 – a move which prompted its permanent reopening, with an appropriate reorganisation of local bus services, in January 1981, with aid from Derbyshire County Council. Local trains call here but Expresses hurry past on the climb to Bradway Tunnel, bored over 2000 yards through the millstone grit to gain access to the Sheaf Valley and a direct approach to the steel city of Sheffield. Dore has no platform on the main line tracks. A few Expresses diverge just south of Dore Station to reach Manchester without running into and out of Sheffield. As the train slows for the journey's end, the well-kept Victorian stone station contrasts starkly with the massive twentieth-century Park Hill flats complex on the slopes above.

The city of Sheffield, with 547,000 inhabitants, until recently the centre of the cutlery trade and the steel industry, owes its origins to the existence of coal, ganister, fireclay and millstone grit as well as fast-flowing streams all in close proximity. The cutlery trade was established in the sixteenth century and in about 1740 Huntsman produced the first crucible steel using local fireclay for making the pots in which the steel was smelted. In the same period, Thomas Boulsouver discovered the process of silverplating copper to produce Old Sheffield Plate.

The topography of the district meant that Sheffield was first served by a branch line from the North Midland Railway at Rotherham; but later construction has turned it into today's important junction, with services to the north-east, south-west, Lancashire, Humberside and East Anglia, as well as the Main Line from London St Pancras.

MANSFIELD AND SHERWOOD FOREST
by Malcolm Goodall

'Near this stone grew a tree reputed to be the centre of the Ancient Forest of Shirwood', states the inscription on a stone in Westgate, Mansfield, near the junction with St John Street.

Mansfield today is a thriving community of 58,000 people, Sherwood Forest an internationally famous tourist attraction, and heavy coal trains trundle across the 15-arch viaduct high above the town centre – but it is more than 20 years since passenger trains last called at the station.

Local authorities are studying the economics of a fast Sprinter service between Nottingham and Mansfield, passing through Hucknall, and with a short piece of new construction at Robin Hood's Hills, in an effort to regenerate the local economy, badly hit by factory and colliery closures. At present, Mansfield has bus services to Alfreton and Mansfield Parkway, but annoyingly, regular buses to Nottingham, Chesterfield and Newark do not serve the main railway stations. There is a service to Newark Castle passing the Minster at Southwell.

Mansfield has a large shopping centre, including a colourful open market (Monday, Thursday, Friday and Saturday), a museum, a civic theatre and arts centre, an indoor leisure centre, a triple screen cinema and good range of clubs, pubs and restaurants.

In 1985 the Robin Hood Way footpath was inaugurated, starting at Nottingham Castle and winding for over 80 circuitous miles through Sherwood to the visitor centre at Edwinstowe, which is set amid relict woodland and stagshead oaks. You can also explore the remains of Sherwood Forest by bicycle from various railheads. Particularly recommended are Clumber Park (see page 32), Newstead Abbey (home of the Byron family) and the ruins of the twelfth-century Rufford Abbey. Buses run every day from Mansfield and Nottingham Victoria bus stations to Rufford and Edwinstowe. Robin Hood no longer waylays travellers, but the Sheriff of Nottingham is still alive and well!

SHEFFIELD–STOCKPORT
(The Hope Valley Line)
by Denis Bradbury

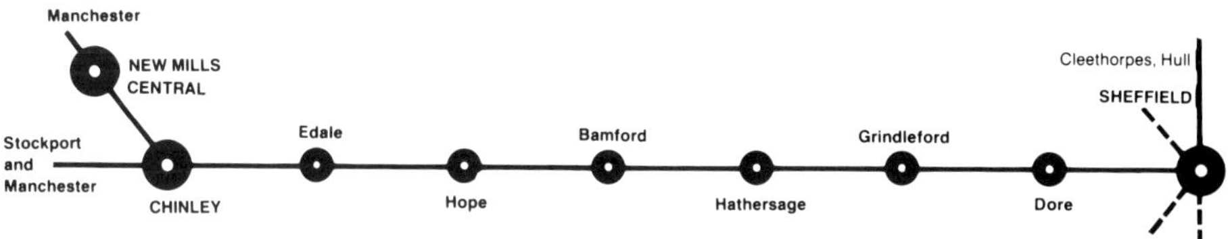

Express trains from East Anglia and Nottingham to Manchester and the north-west reverse from Sheffield back along the incoming route to Dore, where the Hope Valley line branches off, continuing to climb at a steady gradient of 1 in 100 to the summit in Totley Tunnel.

Dore Station, formerly Dore & Totley Station, was once an important junction, but has been reduced to a single platform. The station was built following an agreement between the Duke of Devonshire, who owned most of the surrounding land, and the Midland Railway.

A mile away up the hill to the right of the line is the village of Dore. In the year 827, a treaty was signed here between Egbert, king of Mercia, and Eanred, king of Northumbria, which made Egbert king of the whole English-speaking race from the Firth of Forth to the English Channel, and thus brought about the union of England.

About 1½ miles beyond Dore Station the train enters Totley Tunnel. A board at the entrance states that the tunnel is 6230 yards long, the second longest tunnel in Britain. It took four years to build, the navvies working on it having to contend with vast quantities of water; at one time during the construction, 26,000 gallons were being pumped out every hour. It was said that every navvy working in the tunnel was like Moses – whenever he struck the rock, water gushed out. Water is still a considerable problem in the tunnel today, involving British Rail in a good deal of maintenance.

Apart from the water troubles, the major landowners under whose land the tunnel was driven had to be placated. The Duke of Rutland claimed that the tunnel would interfere with his grouse-shooting on the moors above, and all work in the tunnel was suspended between 12 August and 1 October – the shooting season.

The train emerges from the tunnel at Grindleford in the Derwent Valley. Above this village, millstones were cut out of the rock and sold all over the country to grind grain. Unfinished stones can still be found in various quarries. Grindleford is the first of several North Derbyshire stations on the line at which, particularly at weekends, you can see city-dwellers alighting with rucksacks and walking boots to explore the moors and dales. On the right-hand side near the station is Padley Chapel – a stone building used for many years as a cattle shed. The chapel belonged to Padley Hall, the seat of the Eyre family who were staunch Catholics.

In 1588, during a search, two Catholic priests were found hiding in the hall. They were taken to Derby and hanged, drawn and quartered for the crime of being priests and thus traitors to Queen Elizabeth I. John Fitzherbert, who was living in the hall at the time, was also put to death and the estates confiscated.

From Grindleford the line turns northwards alongside the River Derwent to Hathersage – a pleasant little town which is mentioned in Charlotte Brontë's

Locomotive 47512 emerges from Cowburn Tunnel with an Inter-City train.
(*Photo:* Tom Heavyside)

Jane Eyre under the name of Morton. In Hathersage can be seen the grave of
'Little John', friend of Robin Hood. The grave is some 10 feet long.

The next station along the line is Bamford, where the train crosses the River
Derwent as it flows from the Derwent Valley Water Board's reservoirs a few miles
to the north. The reservoirs, which extend for some six miles up the valley, supply
water to Sheffield, Derby, Nottingham and Leicester. Ladybower, the nearest
reservoir, is about 2 miles from Bamford Station and the dam can be seen briefly
from the train.

Some two miles west of Bamford is Hope, which is also the station for Castleton,
and a reasonably frequent bus service runs between the two.

The limestone hills surrounding Castleton contain four interesting sets of caves.
These comprise the Peak Cavern the Treak Cavern, the Speedwell mine – which
is visited by a trip in a boat along an underground canal built to drain water from
the mine, and higher up on the hillside the Blue John Mine where the famous
Blue John rock is obtained. Above Castleton stands the ruin of Peveril Castle,
dating from the time of William the Conqueror and woven into Scott's *Peveril of
the Peak.*

From Hope Station the line climbs on a steady gradient of 1 in 100 to the
summit in Cowburn Tunnel, following the course of the River Noe. As the line
leaves Hope, a freight branch runs off to the left on its way to Earl's cement works
on the far side of the valley. The works can be seen in the distance, the 300-foot
chimney being one of the tallest in England.

At the head of the valley is Edale Station, a favourite centre for tourists and
hikers and the southern end of the Pennine Way, which stretches for some 250
miles along the summit of the Pennines to Kirk Yetholm on the northern slopes
of the Cheviots.

Beyond Edale village is Kinder Scout, generally known as 'The Peak'. It is a
featureless plateau of heather and peat, several square miles in area, and 2088

feet above sea level at its highest point. No place to be caught in a mist without a compass and map! Here mention may be made of the 'Mass Trespass' by hundreds of people onto Kinder Scout on 4 April 1932 in support of the Access to Mountains Bill, which has been regularly rejected by Parliament since it was first introduced in 1888. The demonstrators were met by a strong force of police and gamekeepers. Five ramblers were arrested and sentenced at Derby Assizes to between two and six months' imprisonment. The Bill finally became law some years later and opened the moorlands to the public for the greater part of the year.

The traveller may well wonder why a flat-topped hill should be called 'The Peak'. The name of the Peak District given to this part of the Pennines has nothing to do with the shape of the hills, but derives from Pecsetan, the name of the Celtic tribe who lived in this area in pre-Roman times. Over the centuries, Pecsetan was changed into Peak.

Shortly after leaving Edale, the train enters Cowburn Tunnel, 3702 yards long and 875 feet below the moor. It has the distinction of being the deepest tunnel on any British railway. One night during the 1914–18 war, the driver and fireman of a train approaching Cowburn Tunnel realised that they were being shadowed by a German Zeppelin. Once the train had entered the tunnel it came to a halt and remained in the tunnel for a considerable time until the loco crew were satisfied that the Zeppelin, having lost the train, had gone away.

From the western portal of Cowburn Tunnel, the train travels a further three miles to Chinley, passing the triangular junction with the former Midland main line to Derby on the left. This line now goes to Buxton only and is heavily used by freight from the extensive ICI limestone quarries at Peak Dale. In summer this route is used by weekend services in connection with Peak Rail's Preservation scheme at Buxton.

As the Hope Valley train approaches Chinley Station, one can look back on the right-hand side and see the Cowburn Tunnel ventilator, high up on the moorland skyline. Chinley Station, 700 feet above sea level, must rank as one of the coldest in the country on which to wait for a train.

Trains to Stockport, Manchester and beyond have since May 1986 taken the left-hand fork, which plunges into the gloom of yet another long tunnel (Disley, 3866 yards) and over a new chord line at Hazel Grove to Stockport (where Buxton line trains also call), Manchester and Liverpool. This modest investment by British Rail sensibly knits together uncoordinated lines inherited from competing companies.

Derbyshire has now been left behind and the train has reached Greater Manchester. Routes and places of interest west of here are described in our companion volume, *Peaks and Plains by Rail.*

DERBY–SHEFFIELD
(Midland Main Line)
by Malcolm Goodall

The second major InterCity route in the area covered by this book runs from Derby north-eastwards to Sheffield. Long-distance trains from the west and Birmingham to Yorkshire and the north-east are joined by High Speed Trains from London to Sheffield. For the first $10\frac{1}{2}$ miles north of Derby, the line travels up the valley of the River Derwent, which it crosses several times, passing through Duffield and the deep cutting through Belper, with its numerous bridges, to

Ambergate, where the route to Matlock diverges. As main-line trains run non-stop over this section, it is covered in greater detail on page 58.

The junction at Ambergate was originally a triangular one and the station had three sets of platforms. Now it has only one platform for the Matlock trains, which diverge to the left, while the main line leaves the Derwent Valley, burrows through two short tunnels and heads up the valley of the River Amber.

The remains of Wingfield Manor then command the skyline over the valley on the west. South Wingfield village on the hilltop overlooks the church by the closed station. The classically-designed booking hall still survives, though now blackened and neglected; its designer, Francis Thompson, spared no expense in producing this and other small gems of architecture.

The escarpment on the east side is the outcrop of the coal measures; one small drift mine driven straight into the scarp is still active, but other collieries around here are worked out and the mineral is mined at deeper levels further east. The Roman road, Ryknild Street, ran along the ridge between Derby and Chesterfield, surveyed in straight lines from one hilltop to another regardless of gradients; but the railway hugs the valley bottom until it has to resort to tunnelling through the watershed under the small town of Clay Cross. One of the earliest electric telegraphs on a railway was installed here as long ago as 1841 to give communication between both ends of the tunnel. Rich coal seams discovered during tunnelling led to the formation of the Clay Cross Company for mining and iron smelting.

At Clay Cross, the main line is joined by the later Erewash Valley route from Nottingham, and from there to Sheffield is described on page 50.

The crooked spire of
All Saints Church, Chesterfield.
(*Photo:* Malcolm Goodall)

CITY OF DERBY
by Simon Hartropp

Now that Derby is an open station, here is a 1-hour alternative to watching other people's trains come and go while you wait for yours.

Turn right out of the station into Station Approach. Pause to look behind you at the Midland Railway crest. How many town and city badges can you recognize? Around you are reminders of the years when 'the railway' provided work, rest and play for its employees. BR Staff Association still runs the imposing Institute, a building with facilities for a whole range of social and educational activities. At the end of the car park is a feature of the old Derby Station – the clock with the Midland Railway crest.

Past the Institute, an entire hamlet of Midland Railway cottages has been restored by the Derbyshire Historic Buildings Trust. The soundness of the basic structures was a tribute to the original builders – but the plasterwork left a lot to be desired!

At the end of the main row is the inevitable public house, but its name and the 'Canal St' name-plate give clues to an earlier transport interchange. The Derby Canal gave access to the national waterways network via the Trent & Mersey Canal. Most of it has been filled in, but if you take the footpath off to the right (signposted 'Recreation Ground'), a new metal footbridge crosses over one of the old cuts. This one was left to provide essential drainage – nowadays it runs directly into the River Derwent. Bass was one of those nineteenth-century benevolent dignitaries who took an interest not only in his business but also civic affairs. His statue stands outside the Derby Museum. Today this green park is the venue for travelling fairs.

Continue towards the city centre over the undulating ground until you reach the large Cockpit roundabout. Site of a very ancient sport (happily now banned), and the old Derby Ice Factory (vital in the days before fridges were available), it carries the inner ring road traffic away from the shopping district. Turn left along (lower) Traffic Street, following the signposts for Loughborough (A6). Look across the dual carriageway to view the Derby Playhouse complex, and the Eagle Centre (if you have time, and want to look around, there is a pedestrian underpass into the Eagle Centre). Continue along Traffic Street until you reach London Road. If it's spring time look straight ahead up the hill to admire the display of naturalised bulb flowers in the verge. Turn left into London Road. Set back behind traditional iron railings are the Liversage Almshouses. Even though there is no vehicular access, they continue to be popular as they are well-maintained by the Liversage Charity. Prospective residents cannot just apply; they must be recommended to the trustees.

Continue past the modern-fronted Queens Hall Methodist Mission until you reach the traffic lights. Turn left into Midland Road, and see the new, automated General Post Office. Derby is a major mail centre, for eight travelling Post Offices pass through its railway station each night, and the East Midlands airport, only 11 miles away, is the hub of first class airmail services in the UK.

Near the station is the War Memorial, let into the wall of the Midland Hotel. If you are thinking of a week's holiday, perhaps using one of the BR Railtourer tickets (Midlands, East Midlands, North Midlands), then call in at the clutch of hotels opposite the station for tariffs – any one would make a good base.

SINFIN–DERBY–MATLOCK
by Simon Hartropp and Harry Pearson

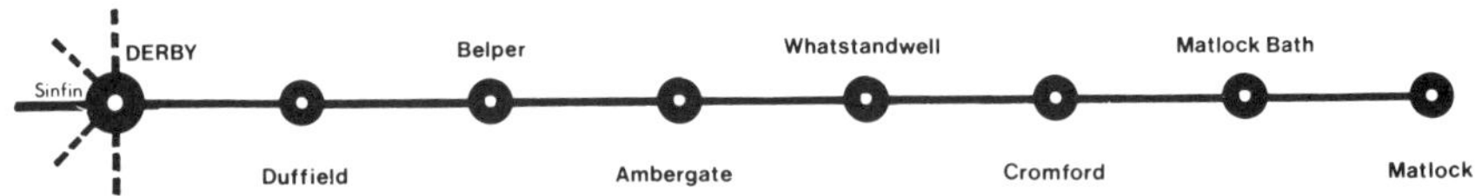

The short Sinfin branch was reopened in 1976 as an ambitious scheme by the county council to relieve traffic congestion by enabling the many commuters from north of Derby to reach the factories to the south. Typically there are just three trains on workdays.

The train sets out from Sinfin Central Station. This site was a 'mock town' in World War II, set up to divert bombers from the Rolls-Royce works, railway and other prime targets a mile or two away. Now the mock town has been replaced by the very solid structures of the Rolls-Royce design offices, engine development and assembly buildings, and one of the most modern foundries in the world.

First stop is Sinfin North. Tucked in between Qualcast and NEI International Combustion, this station is, I think, unique in Britain as it does not have any public access – one can only walk to the adjacent factories.

Now the train curves tightly to the right, joins the main line from Birmingham and passes under the ring road. We stop at Peartree Station, convenient for Smith's non-ferrous foundry and the Rolls-Royce 'main works' and materials laboratories. As the train leaves Peartree, look over to the left and you'll see the floodlights of the famous Baseball Ground – home of Derby County Football Club. We are in the district of the forge, foundry and factory. Almost any British transport vehicle has had some part made here. In passing look for Rolls-Royce (aircraft engines), Ley's Castings (cars), Williams group, and BREL (1988) Ltd. (coaches). We go under the London Road bridge, and to out left admire the stone 'Derby' implanted in an attractive flower bed by the modern power signal-box.

Leaving Derby, the journey to Duffield is soon over. But if going further there is ample time to enjoy the open view across the valley of the Derwent to Allestree and as far as the water tower at Quarndon which is a landmark for some miles around. The view of Eaton and Duffield Bank on the other side makes you understand why this is a very pleasant place to live, and perhaps explains the extent of the platforms at Duffield Station. I wonder how many people remember that there was once another railway up Duffield Bank, built by Sir Arthur Heywood for his own amusement to about one quarter scale with station, signalling bridges, tunnels etc? It was all sold and removed in 1915. What an attraction that would now be!

From Duffield a branch single line runs to Wirksworth. Unfortunately it now carries only minimal freight traffic and occasional Wirksworth Phoenix special trains from Derby to the spring bank holiday well-dressings at Wirksworth. Don't miss a chance to travel by such a rare route to a colourful and historic event.

Incidentally the line here was built by George Stephenson for the North Midland Railway Company in 1839 necessitating re-arrangement of the turnpike road between Duffield and Milford and the building of the Milford Tunnel to Belper. When it was opened on 11 May 1840 a great feast for all the workmen took place in a field in Duffield!

If you are quick you can see the sighting tower up on the Chevin that was erected to facilitate the building of the Milford Tunnel. Out of the tunnel we cross over the Derwent again, (how many times does the railway bridge the River

Derwent between Derby and Matlock?) and run under so many bridges to Belper Station. This is placed centrally in the present town, though when the station was built the town was higher up, where it was supposedly healthier.

The railway through Belper is in a deep cutting, but it soon leaves this for the openness of the run to Ambergate, crossing the Derwent four times before it gets there. So far we have been running along the main line to Sheffield and the north but from here the line to Matlock branches off to the left. Some time ago this route was still the main Midland route to Manchester but now it is single track and goes only as far as Matlock. From Ambergate you will have the experience of travelling along a quite narrow valley with the Cromford Canal, the railway, the main A6 road and the River Derwent parallel, all the way to Cromford. There must be few places left where this can still be seen. The canal is a haven for wildlife and a most enjoyable walk is the 5 or 6 miles from Ambergate to Cromford along the canal tow-path, or half the way to Whatstandwell.

Between Whatstandwell and Cromford the four routes mentioned above change their order in a quite confusing way. The railway crosses over the river four times, and the canal actually crosses the river by the Wigwell aqueduct. Almost immediately after this you pass the Leawood pump-house which pumped water for the canal, and then the remains of High Peak Junction. This was the start of the High Peak Railway – wagons being hauled up the steep slopes by cables to Middleton Top (where you can still see an engine house in pseudo-action) and then proceeding as far as Whaley Bridge. There are benches and tables here which make it a convenient stop for refreshment on the canal walk.

There is a great deal of interest in Cromford, though the station is some distance from the village. The Arkwright Society has published excellent and cheap guides to both the village and the canal, and has taken over the original Arkwright Cromford Mill, where many such guides can be purchased. If you look round Cromford apart from the canal wharf and the mills, do not fail to visit North Street to see what wonderful houses Arkwright built for his workers. If you are interested in books, particularly second-hand, then you should visit the Scarthin Bookshop just up Scarthin Nick from the Market Place.

From Cromford you can also walk over the heights on the left of the road and river, or over High Tor on the right, one of the above guides being for this purpose.

The railway goes into a tunnel most of the way to Matlock Bath, but opens out in a comprehensive view of Matlock town before entering Matlock Station and the end of our journey.

Look at the architecture of Cromford and Matlock Bath stations. Matlock Bath was to be the Switzerland of England when the railway was built, and the station architecture reflects this.

The advantages of a railway link between Derby and Matlock are so obvious that it may seem trite to restate them, but we are so accustomed to travel by road that they are often overlooked on short journeys. There is a smooth uninterrupted ride which is relatively fast – 7 minutes to Duffield, 11 minutes to Belper and 31 minutes to Matlock. And the frequency of the service is sufficient for many purposes (fifteen trains daily Monday to Saturday, fewer on Sundays). Moreover the cost is competitive with other forms of transport. Anyone can use the 'Derbyshire Wayfarer' ticket, or if you are retired you can use a senior citizens' card at half price.

The attractions of this valley route make excursions along it doubly enjoyable. If you drive, you cannot see much else than the road ahead, but the scenery from the railway is well worth looking at: also wherever you leave the car, there you have to return, whereas one of the delights of the valley is to walk along the route from one point to another without having to retrace steps.

WHAT TO SEE AND DO ALONG THE MATLOCK BRANCH

Few branch lines contain so much of interest in such a small catchment area, amid such attractive scenery as the $6\frac{3}{4}$ miles from Ambergate to Matlock.

WHATSTANDWELL

This is the nearest station to the National Tramway Museum at Crich, a mile away up a steep hill. Leave the station by the footbridge, turn right at the road then left up a narrow road through Crich Carr. A collection of 40 tramcars from Britain and overseas is accommodated in a former quarry, with several available for visitors to ride along a 1-mile tramway with fine views. Open Easter – October at weekends and Monday–Thursday May–September. For details contact the National Tramway Museum, Crich, Matlock, DE4 5DP (telephone (0773) 852565). There is an hourly bus service from Matlock. Just round the corner from the tramway museum is Crich Stand. Erected as a war memorial to the Sherwood Foresters Regiment, it is usually open. The view from its top is breathtaking – but beware of the wind!

If you alight from a tram at Wakebridge you are well on the way to Florence Nightingale's birthplace at Holloway, and $3\frac{1}{2}$ acres of Lea Rhododendron Gardens.

CROMFORD

Cromford Mill, the world's first successful water-powered cotton spinning mill built by Richard Arkwright in 1771, is open Wednesdays, Thursdays, Fridays and Sundays all year plus summer Saturdays (telephone (0629) 824297).

Cromford Wharf Steam Museum has a collection of stationary steam engines.

On summer Saturday and Sunday afternoons, horse-drawn barge trips are operated along the Cromford Canal to Leawood Pumping Station, where the pumps are occasionally steamed during the summer.

High Peak Trail is a $17\frac{1}{2}$-mile-long walk and cycle-way from High Peak Junction, near Cromford, to Dowlow near Buxton, much of it on the trackbed of the Cromford & High Peak Railway, closed in 1967. Former railway workshops at High Peak Junction are open to the public at weekends, bank holidays and in school holidays. Three miles (and two inclines) along the trail is Middleton Top with a magnificent viewpoint, bookstall, cine-corner, cycle ride and – at peak times – restored steam engine.

MATLOCK BATH

Take a cable car to the Heights of Abraham Tree Tops Visitor Centre, Prospect Tower, Great Rutland Cavern and Nestus Mine, open daily Easter–October, plus restricted opening times in winter (telephone (0629) 2365).

Derbyshire Toy Museum is open Easter–September, afternoons except Fridays, and on winter Sunday afternoons.

Peak District Mining Museum is open daily all year.

Gulliver's Kingdom – open daily March–September – is a theme park designed for families with younger children.

The Aquarium – with many species of British and tropical fish – is open daily Easter–September and winter weekends.

Illuminations at the Derwent Pleasure Grounds in the autumn rival the more famous ones in Blackpool!

MATLOCK

Hall Leys Park lies alongside the River Derwent, with gardens, tennis, bowls, crazy golf, miniature railway. Also in the town, visit the fifteenth-century parish church.

Riber Castle is a ruin on the hill to the south of the town, with wildlife park, model railway, car museum and children's playground, open daily all year.

For further exploration of the Dales, or visits to Haddon Hall or Chatsworth House, Matlock bus station is 2 minutes' walk from the railway station. Come out of the station approach, cross the river and bear left.

Matlock Railway Station contains a buffet and bookshop operated by Peak Rail – the preservation society re-laying the line from here to Buxton – and a small exhibition.

For full information contact Derbyshire Dales District Council, Tourist Information Office, The Pavilion, Matlock Bath, DE4 3NR (Telephone 0629–55082).

PEAK RAIL
by John Snell
(Managing Director, Peak Rail plc)

Peak Rail was formed in the mid-1970s with the aim of reconstructing and operating the closed section of the Midland Railway's Derby–Manchester route between Matlock and Buxton. The organisation comprised an enthusiast society, the Peak Rail Society with a membership of approximately 1500, and an operating company, Peak Rail plc, which has some 3,000 shareholders.

Peak Rail owns the 3-acre Buxton Midland Station site where a thriving steam centre has been established. The company also leases land and buildings from BR and Derbyshire Dales District Council at Matlock station, where a shop, café and loco restoration building have been developed; and from Derbyshire Dales District Council at Darley Dale where the up-side station building and platform have been renovated.

In 1979–81, Peak Rail operated a charter public Sunday service on the Derby–Matlock line. This demonstrated the viability of the service and in 1982 it was taken over on a revenue support basis by Derbyshire County Council. From 1983 to date it has been wholly operated by BR, without any revenue support.

The section of the Matlock–Buxton line between Buxton and Blackwell Mill ($3\frac{3}{4}$ miles) is still operated by BR as a freight line to service the extensive quarries between Blackwell Mill and Chinley. In 1985, Peak Rail operated a profit-sharing DMU service with BR over this line as part of a Buxton–New Mills Central public service on Sundays, making connections with Hope Valley trains. The service, called 'The Peak Rail Rambler', was extremely successful and did not need to call on the revenue guarantee offered by Derbyshire County Council. The 'Rambler' continued as a Peak Rail charter in 1986, and in 1987 was able to call at a new rambler's halt called Chee Dale at Blackwell Mill. There were no trains in 1988 because of resignalling requirements, but a resumption of service was expected for the 1989 season.

At Buxton, a grant of £30,000 was received from Greater Manchester Council to assist in replacing the missing bridge which separated Buxton Midland Station from the Ashwood Dale line. This project now enables the 'Rambler' service to operate from Midland Station.

In the late 1970s and early 1980s Peak Rail had been repeatedly frustrated in its attempts to obtain planning permission for the entire 20-mile route from Buxton to Matlock, the authorities being concerned that the restricted road access and limited parking provision of the original railway would be inadequate for the scale of tourist project necessary to sustain the new line. However tenacity, persistence and patience on the part of the company and the society paid off, despite environmental considerations. First a temporary permission for the Matlock to Darley Dale section was obtained, then success at a public inquiry resulted in the scheme being written into the Matlock Local Plan. The parking problem was overcome with a proposal for a major visitor centre with new road access off the A6 near Rowsley, and permission for the whole route was obtained in mid-1988.

The local authorities, who own most of the trackbed, finally accepted a financial and operating plan based on a 15-year reconstruction period using mainly volunteer labour, supported by a series of Public Share Issues to match available grant aid. Each stage will have a clearly defined objective and be financially self-sufficient on completion. The first Public Share Issue was launched in late October 1988, with a minimum target of £35,000. Forty days later over £130,000 had been subscribed, with the result that by early December 1988 trackbed clearance was complete between Matlock and Darley Dale and the base layer of ballast for tracklaying was being spread.

With Buxton Midland Station soon to be fully equipped to receive, service and turn visiting steam excursions and host charter trains, and with line reinstatement steadily progressing northwards from Matlock, it looks at least as if the Peak Rail dream now has a very good chance of becoming reality.

COME AND JOIN US!

The Railway Development Society is a national, voluntary, independent body which campaigns for better rail services, for both passengers and freight, and greater use of rail transport.

It publishes books and papers, holds meetings and exhibitions, sometimes runs special trains and endeavours to put the case for rail to politicians, civil servants, commerce and industry and the public generally, as well as feeding users' comments and suggestions to British Rail management and unions.

Membership is open to all who are in general agreement with the aims of the Society and subscriptions (May 1989) are:

Standard rate: **£7.50**

Reduced rate (for pensioners, full-time students): **£4**

Families: **£7.50** plus £1 for each member of household

Special rates also apply for corporate bodies.

Write to the Membership Secretary, Mr F. J. Hastilow, 49 Irnham Road, Four Oaks, Sutton Coldfield, West Midlands B74 2TQ.

The Lincolnshire branch of the society covers Lincolnshire and South Humberside. Its acting secretary is John Saunders, Stockwell Gate, Whaplode PE12 6UE.

The North Midlands branch covers Nottinghamshire and Derbyshire. Its secretary is Mr R. M. Goodall, Albemarle Cottage, Kirklington Road, Eakring, Newark, Nottinghamshire NG22 0DA.

There are many local rail users' groups, the majority of whom are affiliated to the Railway Development Society. Those in the area covered by this book include:

Matlock–Sinfin Rail Users' Group. Contact Simon Hartropp, 72 Empress Road, Derby DE3 6TE.

Lincoln–Newark–Nottingham Rail Users' Group. Contact John Pepper, 7 Main Street, Lowdham, Nottingham NG14 7AB.

Hope Valley Rail Users' Group. Contact Dr Hugh Porteous, 115 Wollaton Road, Sheffield.

Peak Rail. Membership Secretary: Mark Packham, 38 Peterborough Road, Lodge Moor, Sheffield S10 4JE.

South East Lincolnshire Travellers' Association. Treasurer: Mr R. L. Waite, 14 Cross Street, Skegness PE25 3RM.

With the exception of Trent's 'Busline', which is by arrangement with Derbyshire County Council, companies will give only details of their own services even though other operators run on the same routes. Refer to County Council publications for smaller operators' services.

Details of *all* buses in Lincolnshire can be obtained by dialling either Lincoln 552222 or Boston 310010 and asking for extension 3135. Timetable leaflets are also available.

Doe's Bus/Rail Guide Gives information about services between railheads and principal non-rail-served destinations throughout the country. It costs £4 (post free) from B. S. Doe, 25 Newmorton Road, Moordown, Bournemouth, Dorset, BH9 3NU. Also available from the same address is *Doe's Directory of Bus Timetables* which lists bus operators on a county-by-county basis and costs £2.

TOURIST INFORMATION CENTRES

ALFRETON:	Library, Severn Square. Tel. (0773) 833199
BAKEWELL:	Old Market Hall, Bridge Street. Tel. (062 981) 3227
BOSTON:	Assembly Rooms, Market Place. Tel. (0205) 56656
CASTLETON:	Tel. Hope Valley (0433) 20679
CHESTERFIELD:	Peacock Heritage & Information Centre, Low Pavement. Tel. (0246) 207777
CLEETHORPES:	Tel: (0472) 200220
DERBY:	Library, Wardwick. Tel. (0332) 31111 ext. 2185, or (0332) 46124
DERBYSHIRE DALES DISTRICT COUNCIL:	The Pavilion, Matlock Bath. Tel. (0629) 55082
EDALE:	Tel: Hope Valley (0433) 70207
GRANTHAM:	St Peters Hill. Tel. (0476) 66444
HECKINGTON:	Pea Room Station Yard. Tel. (0529) 60765
LINCOLN:	Castle Square and Cornhill in the pedestrian precinct. Tel. (0522) 29828
LONG EATON:	Public Library, Tamworth Road, Tel. (0602) 735426
NEWARK-ON-TRENT:	Beastmarket Hill (opposite the castle). Tel. (0636) 78962
NOTTINGHAM:	16 Wheeler Gate. Tel. (0602) 470661
SKEGNESS:	Embassy Centre, Grand Parade. Tel. (0754) 4821
SPALDING:	Ayscoughfee Gardens. Tel. (0775) 5468
STAMFORD:	The Museum, Broad Street. Tel. (0780) 55611

ISBN 0–7117–0447–3
© Railway Development Society 1989
Published by Jarrold Colour Publications Norwich
Printed in Great Britain. 1/89